HIGH-TECH

A Look at Genetically Engineered Foods

HARVEST

by Elizabeth L. Marshall

An Impact Book
Franklin Watts
A Division of Grolier Publishing
New York • London • Hong Kong • Sydney
Danbury, Connecticut

For Jeff, Abigail, and Amanda

Visit Franklin Watts on the Internet at:
http://publishing.grolier.com

Photographs ©: AP/Wide World Photos: 14 (Richard E. Drew), 18 (Mark Elias), 74 (PA); Dr. R. L. Brinster: 35; Dr. Zhanjiong: 69; Monkmeyer: 104 (Betty Press); Monsanto: 54; Photo Researchers: 65 (Bill Bachman), 109 (Holt Studios International/Nigel Cattlin), 98 (Lynn Lennon), 11 (Rosenfeld Images, Ltd./SPL); Runk/Schoenberger: 51 (Grant Heilman); Superstock, Inc.: cover.

Illustrations by Bob Italiano and George Stewart

Library of Congress Cataloging-in-Publication Data

Marshall, Elizabeth L.
    High-tech harvest: a look at genetically engineered foods/ Elizabeth L. Marshall.
    p. cm. — (An Impact book)
    Includes bibliographical references and index.
    Summary: An overview of recombinant DNA technology, or genetic engineering, techniques used to create crop plants and farm animals with characteristics that are attractive to farmers, food processors, and consumers.
    ISBN 0-531-11434-1
    1. Agricultural biotechnology—Juvenile literature. 2. Food— Biotechnology—Juvenile literature. [1. Agricultural biotechnology. 2. Genetic engineering. 3. Food—Biotechnology.] I. Title. II. Series.
S494.5.B563M368   1999
641.3—dc21   98-8203
                                                                  CIP
                                                                   AC

©1999 by Elizabeth L. Marshall
All rights reserved. Published simultaneously in Canada.
Printed in the United States of America.
    3 4 5 6 7 8 9 10 R 08 07 06 05 04 03 02 01 00

CONTENTS

ACKNOWLEDGMENTS

Thanks to Dan Halacy for initiating this project. I benefited from his original outline. Thanks are also due to Thomas M. Zinnen, Ph.D., biotechnology education specialist at the Biotechnology Center, University of Wisconsin, Madison, for commenting on a draft of this manuscript. Finally, thank you to my father, William E. Marshall, Ph.D., for sharing his expertise with me as I worked on this book and to Deb Goldberg Gray and Julian Goldberg for hosting me while I was in California.

-Introduction-
BRAVE NEW FOODS

What do you get when you cross a tomato with a fish?

A tomato that still tastes delicious after it sits in the refrigerator, of course!

The tomato-fish cross isn't really a true cross. (Fish and tomatoes can't be convinced to reproduce together, after all.) But in the early 1990s, when scientists working at DNA Plant Technology in Oakland, California, wanted to develop a tomato that could be refrigerated without losing its flavor, they thought of using a **gene** from the Arctic flounder, a fish that lives in very cold water. By inserting the Arctic flounder gene into the **genetic material** of a tomato plant, they created a tomato that could be refrigerated and still be tasty.[1]

This experimental tomato is a dramatic example of a genetically engineered food. Although work on the tomato has been abandoned, it stands as a vivid illustration of how we can alter foods to meet our needs. By using the tools and techniques of **genetic engineering** to rearrange genes, or to **splice** genes from one species into another, scientists have learned how to create new varieties of plants. Genetic engineering has also been used to develop new varieties of pigs, sheep, and fish.

Suddenly, the future of agriculture and food production seems limited only by the imagination. Possible foods of the future include:

- Healthier french fries made from potatoes that absorb less oil while frying
- Naturally lean bacon
- Apples loaded with nutrients known to prevent cancer
- Broccoli and brussels sprouts with new, improved tastes
- Bananas that stay ripe for weeks
- Coffee with naturally low amounts of caffeine
- Crops protected against insects and diseases
- Rice that can be grown in poor soil or cold regions

The possibilities seem endless, and so do the questions surrounding this new breed of crops. Will people want to eat these engineered foods? How might such foods change our system of agriculture? Our environment? Our health?

Research in this field began in the 1980s. The first genetically engineered plants were grown outdoors in May 1986.[2] Since then, many millions of dollars have been spent researching how to create genetically engineered tomatoes, corn, soybeans, cotton, and other crops. In the United States, this research is being done by private companies, universities, and the Department of Agriculture.

All that research is now beginning to bear fruit. In fact, the first products of genetic engineering have already been developed. Many more will soon be available. Some experts believe that the world is on the edge of a major agricultural revolution, one that promises to be as far-reaching and significant as the industrial revolution of the 1700s or the computer revolution of the 1980s. Does this mean we'll soon start seeing rot-free bananas or vitamin-packed peppers at the supermarket? Not necessarily. Most laboratory creations will never make it to the dinner table. It's a long, long road from the test tube to the supermarket. Consumer demand—or resistance—plays an important role in what is and isn't sold. One reason DNA Plant Technology stopped work on the tomato with the Arctic flounder gene is that company executives thought shoppers might refuse to buy it.

The appearance of genetically engineered crops has stirred some deep passions. Several consumer and environmental groups have been vocal in their opposition to such foods. Some want to know how these foods will affect our health. Others are concerned about how they affect the environment. Still others have questions about how the development of genetically engineered crops may change the face of agriculture in the United States.

At the other end of the spectrum are those who champion the promise of genetic engineering in agriculture. These people paint a future in which farmers will be able to reduce the amount of chemicals needed to grow crops because the plants will be engineered for protection against insect pests. If crops are engineered to withstand greater heat, cold, drought, or dampness, they could be grown in more parts of the world. World hunger is an enormous problem. Genetically engineered food could be part of the solution, say these advocates.

At the heart of this debate are questions about the potential good and potential harm of these products. Do the benefits outweigh the risks? The Food and

Drug Administration (FDA), the Environmental Protection Agency (EPA), and the United States Department of Agriculture (USDA) are the three government agencies that share responsibility for overseeing this new field in the United States. These agencies evaluate new foods and crops strictly on the basis of safety. Some groups opposed to genetically engineered crops would like U.S. agencies to take a careful look at the social and economic impact of these crops, as European government agencies do when evaluating new products.

Nowhere have the differing viewpoints on genetically engineered foods clashed more violently than on the subject of labeling. Should genetically engineered foods have special labels? Would you want to know if your food contained genetically engineered ingredients? What would the labels say? Is labeling even possible? In general, opponents of these new crops want labels. They believe labels would discourage shoppers from buying the foods. But some supporters want labels too. They believe that labels would help pave the way to consumer acceptance. In 1992, the FDA ruled that labels are not required.

Everyone cares about the food they eat. After all, food is more than just something we eat to stay alive. Food can comfort. Food can celebrate. Food can be given as a token of hospitality or love. It's no wonder that the ability to change the structure of food in a fundamental way has created a great deal of concern and anxiety. Questions about the marriage of genetic engineering and food are important to us all and should be debated in school, in the media, and in shopping malls and town squares across the country. The average person—like you—has an important role to play as this new technology alters the food we eat.

-1-
BRING ON THE NEW FOODS!

The supermarket of the future, in many respects, is already here. You may not realize it, but farmers and food manufacturers are already using genetic engineering to bring you the food you eat.

Did you eat any cheddar cheese today? More than half of the hard cheese currently sold in the United States is made with an **enzyme** called **chymosin**, which is produced by genetically engineered fungi. The rest of the cheese is made with chymosin obtained the traditional way—from a substance known as rennet. Rennet comes from the stomachs of slaughtered calves. Although cheesemakers can use chymosin from either source, the chymosin made from genetically engineered bacteria is easier to obtain and more pure. Approved by the Food and Drug Administration in March 1990, chymosin became the first genetically engineered food ingredient to receive approval in the United States.[1]

Did you drink a glass of milk at today? About 30 percent of the milk produced in the United States comes from cows that have received genetically engi-

Cheese-making requires the ingredient chymosin, obtained either from rennet or from genetically engineered fungi. A worker adds a bowl of rennet to a vat of milk during the cheese-making process.

neered hormones to increase their milk production.[2] Despite the hormone's exotic origins, it is practically identical to the growth hormone that is produced naturally in a cow's body.

You almost certainly will eat a food that contains corn or corn syrup today. These ingredients are found in many processed foods, including breakfast cereals, soda pop, cake mix, and candy. A growing portion of the corn grown in the United States is genetically engineered for insect resistance. The first genetically engineered corn crops were approved for use by the USDA in 1995. They were first grown commercially in large amounts in 1996.

As you can see, a wide variety of products used in food production have been genetically engineered.

They range from the enzyme chymosin to whole foods like corn. The whole foods, in turn, may be eaten as they are, or they may be processed to become ingredients in other food products, like cereal or canned soup. Just as the food available to us is enormously varied, the genetically engineered food available to us is varied as well.

Taking a close look at some of the first food-related products of genetic engineering can offer insight into some of the important issues that have emerged in the public discussion of this new field. A tremendous amount of media attention and public discussion preceded the introduction of **bovine somatotropin**, the hormone that increases milk production in cows, and the Flavr Savr tomato.

Critics of genetic engineering used the introductions of these foods as opportunities to make dire predictions of economic and environmental disaster. Champions of the technology grabbed the same opportunities to argue that genetic engineering would make our food healthier, less expensive, and more abundant. In actuality—and with the important advantage of hindsight—bovine somatotropin has had, at best, only a modest effect on the dairy industry. The unsuccessful introduction of the Flavr Savr tomato proved that low consumer demand and shipping difficulties could doom high-tech foods.

Bovine Growth Hormone

Progress in the dairy industry has always meant one thing: building a better milk cow. Since 1955, the number of dairy cows in the United States has dropped by half, and milk production per cow has more than doubled. The reason? Improvements in the care, feeding, and breeding of dairy cattle. A better understanding of the nutritional needs of cows led to improved cattle feed. Well-nourished cows give more milk. More sophisticated veterinary care has also played a part in increasing milk production.

But improving the genetic makeup of dairy cows through **selective breeding** has had the most dramatic influence on milk output. With selective breeding, and especially the use of **artificial insemination**, farmers can breed cows that produce more milk. Artificial insemination is the practice of collecting sperm from prize bulls, freezing it, and then shipping it for use at dairy farms all over the country. With artificial insemination, the best bulls could father dozens of calves each year.

Despite these advances, the dairy industry continued looking for ways to boost milk production. One possible way, dairy experts knew, was to inject cows with growth hormone. The cows' own growth hormone, produced in the pituitary gland, was known to increase milk production. Efforts to isolate and mass-produce the naturally occurring hormone were underway even before genetic engineering took center stage.

Genetic engineering gave scientists a way to produce bovine growth hormone in large quantities. The veterinary drug, developed by Monsanto (St. Louis, Missouri), was approved for use by the FDA in November 1993 and became available for sale in February 1994. By injecting dairy cows every 2 weeks with the hormone, known commercially as Posilac, farmers could expect to see an increase of up to 15 percent in their cows' milk production. Well-managed farms could anticipate an overall increase in profit, even after subtracting the costs of the drug and the additional feed needed by the herd.

The development of Posilac in the 1980s was accompanied by a tremendous amount of scrutiny. The FDA spent years examining Posilac's effect on human health and cow health. The USDA commissioned many studies that examined how the hormone would affect the dairy industry. Other government agencies also issued reports regarding its safety.

Bovine growth hormone (BGH), also called bovine somatotropin (BST), was among the public's first experience with a genetically engineered product affecting their food, so many people were understandably wary. It was difficult for them to see what benefits, if any, they would realize when they bought and drank the milk.

An activist from the Pure Food Campaign dumps 2 gallons (7.6 L) of milk onto a New York City sidewalk to protest the sale of bovine growth hormone. The genetically engineered hormone, which increases a cow's milk production, became available to farmers in February 1994.

At the same time, an organization known as the Pure Food Campaign was very vocal in its opposition to BST. Headquartered in Washington, D.C., and founded by activist and author Jeremy Rifkin, the Pure Food Campaign argued that BST was detrimental to animal health since it would cause an increase in mastitis, an infection of the udder. (Rifkin is also the author of *Beyond Beef* and the leader of the Beyond Beef Campaign, which advocates eating less beef.)

In the 1980s, a financial crisis caused many small farms in the Midwest to go bankrupt. Many people wondered whether BST would be good, economically, for family farms. They also wondered why the United States needed more milk production when the country already had a surplus. (Surplus milk is bought by the government.) Any boost in milk production would cause milk prices to drop. A drop in prices might seem desirable to shoppers, but it would hurt farmers who were unable or unwilling to increase their milk production with BST.

For these reasons, the National Family Farm Coalition, based in Wisconsin, opposed genetically engineered bovine growth hormone. The coalition predicted that it would hurt small family farms. In 1990, before Posilac was even available, then-governor Tommy Thompson of Wisconsin approved legislation banning the sale or use of BST for 1 year. It was the first prohibition of a genetically engineered product in the United States.[3] Other voices also rose in protest. Ben & Jerry's, the ice cream company headquartered in Burlington, Vermont, vowed to make ice cream only from the milk of cows that had not received Posilac injections.

By 1997, BST had been on the market for 3 years and was being given to about 30 percent of the nation's dairy cows. Contrary to many predictions, milk consumption in the United States remained steady. Furthermore, no drop in the price of milk followed the hormone's introduction. Milk production in the United States increased by 2 percent each year in 1994 and 1995, and then actually dropped in 1996 due to a poor corn crop. (Cattle feed is made from corn.) Although BST obviously had some influence on milk production, its influence was not as strong as some predicted it would be.

What has happened, according to agricultural experts, is that BST has become one of a number of variables, including weather and the corn crop, that influence milk production in the United States.[4] Furthermore, experience has shown that both small and large farms can realize increased profits from BST, provided the farms are well-managed.

Despite its smaller-than-expected impact, the introduction of Posilac demonstrated that the benefits and risks of a new food product must be discussed in terms of environmental safety, animal health, and economics, as well as human health. The public is interested not only in how a product will affect their health and finances, but also in how it will affect the environment, animal health, and farming communities.

The Flavr Savr Tomato

Have you ever noticed that the tomatoes you buy in the supermarket in the winter are less attractive and less tasty than the ones you buy at a local farm stand in the summer? The difficulty with tomatoes is that when they ripen—when they become red and tasty—they also get soft. Soft tomatoes have a shelf life of only 4 to 7 days, which is a problem if they are destined for cross-country shipping. To keep vine-ripened tomatoes fresh, distributors ship them in refrigerated trucks. Unfortunately, refrigeration destroys the tomatoes' flavor. As a result, many supermarket tomatoes are picked when they are green and hard, shipped, and then exposed to **ethylene gas**, which causes them to turn pink—but not red.

Because people want red, tasty tomatoes all year long, Calgene (Davis, California) created a tomato that ripened without getting soft. The company's scientists figured out how to block the action of the gene that tells the tomato to get soft after it ripens. By making changes to just one gene, the scientists could delay the rotting process. As a result, the tomato could remain on the vine longer—which is good for flavor and color—before being harvested, while still remaining firm enough to ship. The Flavr Savr tomato could provide people in northern climates with vine-ripened tomatoes in the winter.

Calgene was the first company to market a whole food created through genetic engineering. It anticipated that the public might be concerned about the process because the technology that made the tomato possible was new To reassure the public, Calgene voluntarily asked the FDA to review the Flavr Savr tomato. The company was acknowledging the risks of introducing a new food without publicly accounting for its safety.

On May 29, 1992, the Flavr Savr tomato became the first genetically engineered whole food to receive approval from the Food and Drug Administration. (With chymosin and bovine growth hormone, you don't eat the genetically engineered organism. With a whole food created through genetic engineering, like this tomato, you do.) The Flavr Savr was intro-

A grocer displays two Flavr Savr tomatoes. The Flavr Savr, called the MacGregor tomato by the scientists who developed it, was the first genetically engineered whole food to receive Food and Drug Administration approval. It was offered for sale in 1994.

duced to shoppers in California and Illinois in 1994. As a pioneer among genetically engineered fruits and vegetables, Calgene's Flavr Savr tomato faced initial public resistance, particularly in the form of a boycott by chefs.

Although the Flavr Savr was able to ride out those protests, it was ultimately done in by other, rather low-tech, problems. For starters, the tomato variety that was engineered by Calgene lacked acceptable yields and disease-resistance in Florida and California—two major tomato-growing areas. The tomato was also unable to tolerate shipping and often arrived soft and bruised. By 1996, the novel tomato had been withdrawn from the market.[5]

Insect-Resistant Crops

Several crops genetically engineered to resist insect infestation were grown commercially for the first time in 1996. Unlike the Flavr Savr tomato, these cotton, potato, and corn plants offered no obvious benefits to consumers. Instead, their new feature was intended to appeal to the farmer.

By adding a gene from a common soil bacterium, called *Bacillus thuringiensis*, scientists found that they could create a plant that produced its own defenses against certain pests. This would decrease the amount of a crop lost to insects. It would also, theoretically, limit the use of **pesticides**. The farmer would realize an overall increase in yield. As long as the profits of the increased yield outweighed the costs of using the new technology, the farmer would benefit financially. These insect-resistant crops will be examined more closely in Chapter 4.

What Genetic Engineering Is

Many people are asking whether genetically engineered food is healthy. They want to know whether it will be good for the environment and good for American farmers. They also want to know whether it will save them money. Unfortunately, it's impossible to answer these questions.

Bovine growth hormone, the Flavr Savr tomato, and insect-resistant corn—besides genetic engineering, what do these products have in common? Not much. That's why it is extremely difficult to look at one specific product and make a comment about genetically engineered food in general. After all, the enzyme chymosin doesn't have much in common with a whole food like a potato, and the dairy industry is very different from the tomato market.

The first wave of products to hit the market illustrates the different uses of genetic engineering in food production. Sometimes genetic engineering is used to improve the foods in ways that appeal to the people who eat them. Produce is better-tasting or stays fresh longer, for instance. In other cases, the changes are designed to appeal to farmers or food processors. In those instances, shoppers may be unaware that their food was genetically modified. You may not care whether the corn syrup in your blueberry muffin was made from a crop genetically engineered to resist insect pests, but you can bet that the farmer responsible for that crop did!

Genetic engineering is a tool. This is an important point to remember. Just as a hammer can be used to make a cabinet, a toy, or a house, genetic engineering can also be used in a variety of ways to make lots of different food products.

Although foods developed through genetic engineering may share some characteristics, they are usually far more different than alike. For this reason, the FDA announced on May 29, 1992, that it would evaluate genetically engineered foods based on their individual safety and nutrition, rather than on the methods used to produce them. In other words, the agency would focus on the product instead of the process. The fact that the food had been genetically engineered would not trigger any special treatment of the product. With this decision, the FDA demonstrated its belief that the foods developed through genetic engineering were as safe as foods developed through other agricultural technologies. The role of the FDA and other government agencies responsible for food safety will be examined in more detail in Chapter 6.

Debates over various genetically engineered foods often include an examination of benefits and risks to the individual and to society. With these discussions, it's useful to acknowledge that well-intentioned and thoughtful people may have different values. A vegetarian, for instance, will not suddenly start eating pork simply because genetic engineering can potentially be used to make meat leaner and more healthy.

In the U.S., the FDA reviews new veterinary drugs like BST with three criteria in mind: Is it safe? Is it effective? Is it made with consistent quality? The potential social and economic impact of the new drug is not considered. In Europe, however, social costs and benefits are considered. This means that crops accepted in the United States may be refused in Europe. Since the U.S. exports crops like corn and soybeans to Europe, such resistance can be costly.

What Genetic Engineering Is Not

Not all future advances in agriculture will come from genetic engineering. Imagine visiting a supermarket in the year 2020. Miniature heads of lettuce look like green tennis balls. Further down the produce aisle sit purple potatoes and white radishes. Next to them are average-looking carrots that carry a premium price because, according to their wrapper, they carry an extra dose of a known cancer-prevention agent.

Over in the meat section are many specialty brands of low-fat, or no-fat, pork, hamburger, and chicken. In the snack section, popcorn that doesn't need butter or salt is on sale. Despite all these oddi-ties, many of the brands of cereals, soups, and pasta are familiar to you from your childhood in the 1980s and 1990s.

Question: Which of these foods were created with help from genetic engineering?
Answer: Perhaps all of them. Perhaps none.

Although genetic engineering may bring us lean-er meat, better-tasting popcorn, and vegetables chock-full of disease-fighting nutrients, other fields of science might very well deliver the same thing. For centuries, ordinary breeding programs have been successfully creating new strains of fruits, vegetables, and livestock. That's how we got many varieties of corn and apples. Potatoes that resist rot and peppers with a shelf life of more than a month were produced by traditional plant breeding. Square tomatoes, bred to work well with machine harvesting, are also the product of traditional breeding. The same is true for seedless grapes. New processed foods are also always under development: just think of the new snack food you ate at a friend's house the other day.

Researchers have also used means other than genetic engineering to create new plant varieties in the laboratory. By treating lettuce seeds with a chem-ical, scientists created miniature lettuce in the early 1990s. Chemicals were also used to produce fruits and vegetables in unfamiliar colors.[6]

In addition, not all plant cell experiments involve genetic engineering. For instance, scientists have looked for natural mutations in single plant cells and grown whole plants from those cells. Traditional plant breeding is then used to develop new plant varieties from the new plants. This process is known as **somaclonal variation**. Another technique, dubbed **embryo rescue**, is used by breeders to cross two plant varieties that would not ordinarily breed together.

It can be difficult to distinguish genetic engineering from other kinds of laboratory manipulation. The way such work is described in the press or on TV often doesn't make it easier. The term **biotechnology**, for instance, is sometimes used to refer specifically to genetic engineering and is sometimes used to refer quite broadly to many types of breeding techniques. In this book, the term genetic engineering refers to the laboratory manipulation of **DNA** (deoxyribonucleic acid), the genetic code. Chapters 2 and 3 will examine how this is done.

-2-
WHAT IS GENETIC ENGINEERING?

Which do you prefer: green Granny Smith apples or red delicious apples? Cherry tomatoes or their larger cousins? How could you even begin choosing between sweet corn on the cob and the kind of corn used for popcorn?

We enjoy many different kinds of apples, tomatoes, corn, and other fruits and vegetables. Different breeds of cattle and chicken fill our farms. This variety is due to centuries of careful breeding. Improvements in agriculture have often resulted from developing new varieties of crops and livestock through selective breeding.

According to archeologists, farmers have been choosing particular plants and animals for planting and breeding for at least 6,000 years. Farmers have long understood that plants with desirable characteristics produce seeds that tend to grow into plants with those same characteristics. The seeds of plants with especially good color, taste, or yield can be expected to produce more of the same. This is also true of animals: strong, healthy animals are likely to produce offspring that are also strong and healthy.

These traditional breeding practices are actually a form of genetic modification that has resulted in many varieties of plants and animals. Although these techniques are relatively low-tech, people have used them successfully for thousands of years. Corn, once an inedible grass, has become a key source of food thanks to selective breeding. Today there are hundreds of varieties of corn, ranging in height from 2 to 12 feet (0.6 to 3.7 m), and in color from blue to maroon to white. Although the tools of genetic engineering are new, the desire to develop new varieties of crops and livestock is not.

So which is the best variety of corn or cattle or cucumber? With all these different varieties, you might expect there to be a clear winner. But that is not the case. One reason that so many different varieties have been carefully cultivated is that each has its own desirable characteristics. One variety of wheat may be well suited to grow in Kansas, while another variety is best for Saskatchewan or North Dakota or West Bengal. One variety of corn may be known for its high yield, while another is prized for its resistance to disease.

In short, different varieties often have different strengths, and it is highly unusual for one variety to have more than one or two strengths. Take cattle, for instance. Certain breeds, such as Holsteins and Guernseys, are known as excellent milk producers. Other breeds, like Herefords and Anguses, are raised for their meat. But no breed is an excellent producer of both milk and meat. For this reason, cattle are bred for either one or the other.

Inbreeding is one way to develop varieties with specific traits. When a plant, such as corn, is allowed to self-pollinate for several generations, the result is an inbred variety. Inbred plants are practically identical in their genetic makeup. (Animals can also be inbred, by allowing them to mate only with close relatives. Laboratory mice are an example of an inbred animal.) Seed companies like Pioneer Hi-Bred (Des Moines, Iowa) and DeKalb Genetics Corporation (DeKalb, Illinois) have developed a number of inbred lines of corn. When these parent lines are crossed, the result is known as a **hybrid**.

Hybrid corn combines the traits of the two parent lines. This combination of traits, which usually includes high yield, is greatly prized. The seed from hybrid corn itself, however, lacks value, since it will contain an unpredictable mix of traits. For this reason, farmers who want high-yielding hybrids must buy corn seed each year from the seed companies that own the inbred parent line. The development of hybrid corn in the 1920s and 1930s boosted the importance of private companies, like Pioneer Hi-Bred and DeKalb, to the corn industry.

Practically all the corn grown in the United States is hybrid corn. In addition, many vegetables, including broccoli, carrots, peppers, and tomatoes are grown from hybrid seeds. Not all plant species can be crossed easily. Because it is difficult to cross wheat, barley, rice, and cotton, hybrid varieties of these species are uncommon.

Selection and **hybridization** are traditional breeding practices used to improve the genetics of agricultural species. Through careful breeding, farmers successfully modified the genetic makeup of cows, for instance, to produce animals that were superior milk producers. Of course, early farmers didn't understand how traits were passed from one generation to the next. Nevertheless, long before the field of genetics even had a name, farmers recognized its importance to their lives. The goals of genetic engineering, then, are the same as those of traditional selective breeding: to improve crops and livestock.

A Review of Basic Genetics

Today, we know that inherited characteristics are determined by the genes carried on our **chromosomes**. During reproduction, chromosomes are passed on to the next generation, with the new organism inheriting half its chromosomes from the female parent and half from the male parent. Chromosomes are tiny threadlike structures present in the nucleus of every plant and animal cell. Different species have different numbers of chromosomes. While humans have 46 chromosomes, most varieties of corn have only 20.

Chromosomes are made of protein and DNA. DNA is the molecule that carries genetic information—the set of instructions that tells a cell how to make or absorb food and water; how to produce proteins, lipids, and sugars; and how to remove wastes.

DNA is made of two long strands of building blocks called **nucleotides**. The strands are twisted together into a structure that looks something like a spiral staircase. Each spiraling double helix consists of four types of nucleotides: guanine (G), cytosine (C), thymine (T), and adenine (A). Your genetic code is determined by the order, or sequence, of nucleotides in a strand of DNA. In other words, you can think of DNA as a code written with four letters.

Your cells read your genetic code as a series of three-letter words. Each triplet of nucleotides contains

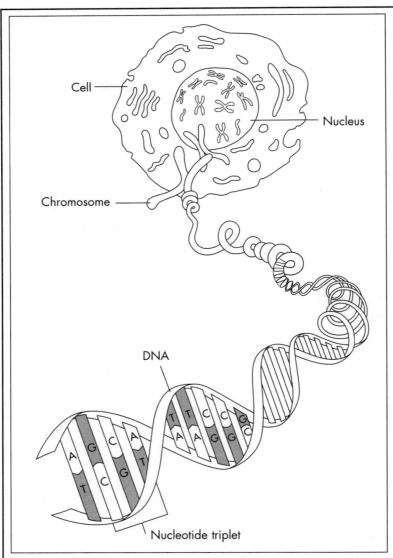

Labels: Cell, Nucleus, Chromosome, DNA, Nucleotide triplet

Chromosomes, present in the nucleus of every plant and animal cell, are made up of protein and DNA. Four different types of nucleotide bases make up DNA: guanine (G), cytosine (C), thymine (T), and adenine (A). A set of three nucleotides is called a triplet.

instructions for building a particular **amino acid**. Amino acids are linked together to build proteins. For example, the nucleotide sequence TATGGT-GTTTCC would be interpreted as four triplets: TAT, GGT, GTT, and TCC. The triplet TAT is a command to obtain the amino acid tyrosine. GGT codes for glycine, GTT codes for valine, and TTC codes for serine. Following DNA's instructions, your cell would produce a protein that consists of tyrosine, glycine, valine, and serine.

	T	C	A	G	
T	Phenylalanine	Serine	Tyrosine	Cysteine	T
	Phenylalanine	Serine	Tyrosine	Cysteine	C
	Leucine	Serine	STOP	STOP	A
	Leucine	Serine	STOP	Tryptophan	G
C	Leucine	Proline	Histidine	Arginine	T
	Leucine	Proline	Histidine	Arginine	C
	Leucine	Proline	Glutamine	Arginine	A
	Leucine	Proline	Glutamine	Arginine	G
A	Isoleucine	Threonine	Asparagine	Serine	T
	Isoleucine	Threonine	Asparagine	Serine	C
	Isoleucine	Threonine	Lysine	Arginine	G
	START	Threonine	Lysine	Arginine	A
G	Valine	Alanine	Aspartic acid	Glycine	T
	Valine	Alanine	Aspartic acid	Glycine	C
	Valine	Alanine	Glutamic acid	Glycine	G
	Valine	Alanine	Glutamic acid	Glycine	A

Each nucleotide triplet codes for a specific amino acid. There are twenty different amino acids. Some triplets signal a start or stop in the DNA sequence. Every living organism uses the same genetic code.

Although sixty-four different triplets are possible with four nucleotides, only twenty kinds of amino acids exist. (Many triplets code for the same amino acid.) Using these twenty amino acids, cells can build more than 50,000 different proteins.

Proteins are the molecules that keep the body running smoothly. Proteins known as enzymes control the chemical reactions of cells. Proteins called hormones regulate growth, reproduction, and other functions. The interaction of many different proteins in your body determines your health, your appearance, and, to some extent, who you are.

The Power of DNA

DNA is the genetic blueprint for all living organisms—from people and petunias to cows and cucumbers. This is an amazing fact, worth stopping to consider for a moment. Think about it: the chemical makeup of DNA is almost exactly the same in every living thing. Even the most gifted biologist can barely distinguish among bacteria DNA, pig DNA, and human DNA. In every species, DNA contains the same four basic ingredients and signals the production of proteins in the same manner.

But wait, you say. Pigs, humans, and bacteria are most certainly different from each other. What gives? Differences between living organisms are governed by differences in the amount of DNA and the order in which the four nucleotides in the DNA are arranged. Variations in the number of chromosomes and the arrangement of nucleotides on those chromosomes account for the variations between species, like ducks and donkeys, and individuals, like you and your sister. Ordering the nucleotides one way gives rise to a human being. Ordering them another way gives rise to a penguin or a paramecium.

So what is a gene? A gene is a segment of DNA that codes for one protein. There are thousands of genes on each chromosome. Some traits—like height and flower color in pea plants—are determined by just one gene coding for one protein. But most traits are determined by the interplay of several genes. Multiple genes coding for multiple proteins result in a characteristic like yield in rice or wool quality in sheep.

An important fact to remember about genes is that many different species share the same genes. This makes sense if you focus on similarities, rather than differences, between species. All mammals breathe air, for instance. The proteins needed for respiration are almost identical in all mammals and, thus, the genes coding for those proteins are also almost identical.

Manipulating DNA: A History

Molecular manipulation is a new twist on the old tried-and-true techniques of selective breeding. Farmers in blue overalls and scientists in white lab coats share a common goal: to build better plants and animals. While farmers use traditional breeding practices to produce offspring with the best qualities of both parents, scientists bypass reproduction altogether. They modify an organism's genetic material directly.

So how do scientists actually do this? How do they rearrange genes or move a gene from one species into another? Can they take a normal corn plant and suddenly turn it into Super Corn? Not exactly.

Scientists cannot change the genetic makeup of full-grown plants or animals. Instead, they must work with seeds or embryos. There are three basic ways of performing genetic engineering.

- In one approach, researchers make changes to an existing gene. For example, they might turn off a gene that controls ripening in tomatoes.
- In another approach, researchers move a gene from one organism into another organism of the same species. Perhaps they want to move a gene from a wild tomato into a variety of domestic tomato.
- In the third approach, scientists move a gene from one organism into an organism of a completely different species. An example of this would be the tomato with the Arctic flounder gene.

Many modern genetic engineering techniques were developed in the 1970s and early 1980s. Before scientists could transfer a gene from one organism to another, they had to learn how to cut a gene out of a chromosome, how to make copies of that gene, and how to insert the gene into a new chromosome. The first experiments in genetic engineering focused on cutting, copying, and splicing DNA segments.

In 1968, scientists discovered **restriction enzymes**, proteins that can be used to cut and splice DNA in specific places. These enzymes are part of bacteria's natural defenses against attacking viruses known as bacteriophages. The restriction enzymes disable the attacking virus by splicing its DNA. More than 400 kinds of restriction enzymes have been identified.

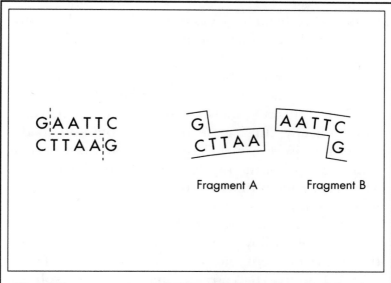

GAATTC
CTTAAG

G
CTTAA

AATTC
G

Fragment A   Fragment B

Restriction enzymes work like chemical scissors. Scientists use them to genetically engineer an organism. One type of restriction enzyme seeks out the sequence GAATTC and cuts it between G and A.

Restriction enzymes work like chemical scissors. They identify specific nucleotides within a DNA strand and cut the strand at that site. For example, one such enzyme seeks out the sequence GAATTC and cuts it between G and A. Restriction enzymes can also be used by scientists to identify genes. Without the discovery of restriction enzymes, genetic engineering would be impossible.

In 1972, Paul Berg, David Jackson, and Robert Symons—three researchers working at Stanford University—did an experiment that showed how restriction enzymes can be used to cut DNA. They also showed that DNA fragments from different organisms can be joined together. In their experiment, DNA from two **microorganisms**—a bacterio-phage and the bacterium *Escherichia coli*—were joined to a monkey virus known as SV40.

A year later, Stanley Cohen at Stanford University, and Herbert Boyer of the University of California at San Francisco, used restriction enzymes to chemically cut a gene out of a common toad's DNA and insert it into *E. coli.* The gene was success-fully taken up by the rapidly reproducing bacterium. The result? Each time the bacterium reproduced, it made copies of its own genes—and the toad gene. This was a tremendous step forward.[1]

The Cohen-Boyer experiment was further proof that restriction enzymes could be used to cut DNA, that different DNA fragments could be spliced together, and that a molecule containing foreign DNA could be duplicated and expressed within *E. coli.* The beginning of the field of genetic engineering is often traced to this experiment.

In 1975, splicing gene fragments together became easier with the discovery of another group of enzymes, known as **ligases**. If restriction enzymes were the scissors of genetic engineering, then DNA ligases were the paste. Now scientists had the tools they needed to cut, paste, and copy genes.

With these new tools, scientists could imagine manipulating the genes of an organism. And if that weren't remarkable enough, they could even envision moving genes from one organism into another of a different species. Scientists began to call plants and animals that contain DNA from another species **transgenic**. This aspect of genetic engineering cap-tured the public's attention. Suddenly, it seemed, sci-ence could create new living things. The ability to move genes across species raised fears and questions. Some critics accused **genetic engineers** of "playing God."

In December 1982, the first transgenic animal made the cover of *Nature*, a science journal. Three American biochemists—Richard Palmiter, of the University of Washington in Seattle, and Ronald Evans and Neal Birnberg, of the Salk Institute in La Jolla, California—described how they had successfully transferred a rat gene into mice. The gene carried the DNA code for rat growth hormone. The result was a transgenic mouse that grew to be nearly twice the normal size. The experiment marked the beginning of transgenic animals.[2]

These two mice are genetically identical, except that the enormous mouse grew from an egg that had been injected with a gene for rat growth hormone. The two mice appeared on the cover of Nature, *a scientific journal, in December 1982.*

Cohen and Boyer's work had launched a revolution. Palmiter's experiment had confirmed that genetic engineering could be used in animals. Although the kind of work these scientists pioneered is most accurately known as **recombinant DNA technology**, it is popularly known as genetic engineering or biotechnology.

The implications of these early experiments were stunning. Suddenly, previously undreamed of advances in medicine, science, and even manufacturing seemed possible. Agriculture had a new way to improve varieties of plants and animals. Recombinant DNA technology was faster and more precise than traditional selective breeding. Even better, the ability to transfer genes between species made even the most fantastic crosses seem within reach.

Scientists, business executives, and stockholders all saw dollar signs when they looked at biotechnology's future. As a result, the early 1980s saw an explosion of biotechnology companies dedicated to developing new products through recombinant DNA techniques. Although most concentrated on developing pharmaceuticals for humans and animals, many were dedicated to applying genetic engineering to agriculture.

-3-
GENE TRANSFER
TECHNIQUES

Each species—whether it be plant, poultry, livestock, or fish—presents unique challenges to genetic engineers. What works with fish is quite different from what works with sheep. The methods that are successful with one plant may be useless with another. As a result, molecular biologists must carefully tailor their efforts to each particular species.

Despite these differences, the basics of genetic engineering can be reduced to four main steps. To transfer a gene from one organism to another, the research team needs to find:

1. A gene to transfer

2. A single-celled **host organism** capable of growing into an adult. For animals, this would be a fertilized egg. For plants, this would be a single cell taken from any tissue.

3. A way to transfer the gene into the host organism

4. A way to coax the single-celled host organism to grow into an adult

If the goal is to alter a gene that occurs naturally in the DNA of an organism, the steps are similar. The scientist needs to find:

1. A gene to alter

2. A single-celled host organism capable of growing into an adult

3. A way to alter the gene

4. A way to coax the single-celled organism to grow into an adult

This process seems simple enough, but it is riddled with obstacles. Successful gene modification will occur only if the scientists can overcome the problems they encounter along the way.

Step 1: Finding a Gene

Finding a gene to manipulate is harder than it sounds. First, there is the question of numbers. Even a simple organism like a bacterium has several thousand genes. Corn has about 30,000 genes.[1] Animals have tens of thousands of genes. Second, finding a useful gene to modify can be difficult. The ideal gene is one that increases the commercial value of a plant or animal. It's the gene that enables a corn plant to produce more corn per acre, or a cow to produce more milk per pound of feed. High yield is a valuable trait. Other commercially valuable qualities include disease resistance, pest resistance, and **herbicide** resistance. Better taste, increased nutrition, and improved appearance are also desirable qualities.

Unfortunately, many of these valuable traits—particularly yield—are controlled by multiple genes. Although genetics has taken enormous strides forward in the past few decades, scientists are only just beginning to understand how multiple genes work together. Recombinant DNA scientists cannot routinely manipulate multiple genes. Until genetic engineers learn how multiple genes interact, many important characteristics of plants and animals will be outside the scope of genetic engineering.

The first attempts at genetic engineering in agriculture have focused on single-gene traits. Calgene's scientists found that they could delay ripening in tomatoes by engineering a single gene. Palmiter's team found that by transferring a single growth hormone gene from a rat, it could trigger enormous growth in a mouse.

Once scientists identify a gene to manipulate, they must isolate it from a cell by cutting it out of the chromosome with restriction enzymes. Other laboratory techniques are used to make multiple copies, or **clones**, of the DNA segment. Once the segment is cloned, it can be transferred.

In recent years, scientists have created cDNA libraries—collections of cloned DNA (cDNA) segments that can be used to obtain genes that have been isolated. Indeed, a major scientific goal has been to identify the location of genes in all the major food crops and to establish labeled clones of those genes. The process of identifying and locating all of an organism's genes is known as **genomic mapping**. A complete map of an organism's genes tells scientists exactly where each gene is located. Biologists are currently working on maps of the corn **genome**, the rice genome, the tomato genome, and other plant genomes.[2]

These maps will not provide scientists with all the information they need, however. Even after maps are available, it will take many more years to learn what proteins each gene codes for and how groups of genes work together. For example, the role of some genes is simply to tell other genes when to turn on or off. Obviously, a better understanding each gene's purpose would be very helpful.

Step 2: Finding a Single-Celled Host

Once scientists have a gene, they need a host organism to put it into. Scientists cannot change the genetic code of an adult organism. They cannot take a full-grown corn plant or cow and turn it into super corn or super cow. Indeed, they cannot even take a corn seedling or newborn calf and do that. That is why the host organism is almost always a single cell that can grow into an adult. As that first cell divides and the organism grows, the new DNA will be present inside every cell—including its seeds or reproductive cells. Thus, the organism will pass the new DNA onto the next generation.

With plants, it is possible to grow an entire plant from any single cell. In most cases, it doesn't even matter whether that cell comes from the root, the leaf, or the stem. This is because every plant cell is **totipotent**—it has the potential to generate an entirely new plant. With the right mix of nutrients, hormones, light, and temperature, the cell can be convinced to divide and grow into a plant.

Working with animals is much more complicated. Animal cells are generally not totipotent. For many years, scientists believed that once an animal cell **differentiates**—becomes a particular kind of cell, such as a muscle cell or a skin cell or a brain cell—it cannot be used to generate a new individual. In 1997, one experiment proved that this idea was wrong. The birth of Dolly, a cloned lamb created from an adult sheep's mammary cell, showed that a new animal can develop from a single cell. Dolly, and the circumstances of her birth, are examined more closely in Chapter 5.

Step 3: Finding a Way to Transfer or Alter the Gene

Once the gene has been identified and the single-celled host is prepared, the next step is to move the gene into the host. For certain species of plants, including tomatoes, potatoes, cotton, and soybeans, Mother Nature has provided a natural gene transfer system in the form of a soil bacteria known as *Agrobacterium tumefaciens*.

Under natural conditions, *A. tumefaciens* attacks plants by inserting some of its DNA into some of the plant's cells. The transferred bacterial DNA signals the growth of a crown gall tumor in the plant. You may have seen such abnormal growths on the stems of tomato plants.

In the early 1980s, researchers at Monsanto and at institutions in West Germany and Belgium developed a mutant form of *A. tumefaciens*.[3] Using restric-

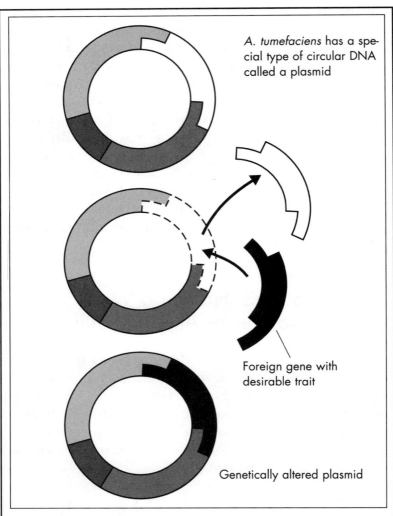

A. *tumefaciens* has a special type of circular DNA called a plasmid

Foreign gene with desirable trait

Genetically altered plasmid

Scientists frequently use the soil bacteria A. tumefaciens *to transfer foreign genes into plants. Scientists can remove part of the* A. tumefaciens *plasmid and replace it with a foreign gene. Now when* A. tumefaciens *transfers some of its own DNA into the plant's cells, the foreign DNA is transferred too.*

tion enzyme and DNA ligase, scientists spliced foreign genes onto the mutant *A. tumefaciens* bacterium. The bacterium, in turn, transferred some of its DNA—including the foreign gene—into the plant cell.

This highly successful method of gene transfer in plants has its limits. Some species of plants, including such important crops as rice, corn, and wheat, are not targets of *A. tumefaciens*.[4] For these crops, scientists had to develop other methods of gene transfer.

These other methods include **gene guns** and a technique called **electroporation**. Believe it or not, gene guns are capable of shooting microscopic gold or tungsten bullets coated with DNA into plant cells. Some of the DNA gets into the chromosomes of the cells. In electroporation, plant cells are suspended in fluids that contain pieces of DNA. When an electric charge is applied, the outer walls of the plant cell are forced open for less than a second. During this brief period, some pieces of DNA wash into the cells.

Transferring a gene into a fertilized egg is far from easy. First, the egg must be removed from the mother's ovary and combined with sperm in the laboratory. Once the egg is fertilized, it is ready to be genetically altered. In most cases, scientists pierce the egg with a tiny needle and insert the new DNA in a process known as **microinjection**. If the egg survives this trauma, it is returned to the uterus of a surrogate mother where it will remain and grow until birth.[5] Since fish eggs are naturally fertilized outside of the body, gene transfer is much more successful in fish than in mammals.

Although the first steps of gene transfer are very time-consuming, they need never be repeated if the experiment is successful. From then on, all the seeds of the transformed plant, or the egg or sperm cells of the animal, will carry the new DNA.

Step 4: Coaxing the Host Organism to Grow

Did the gene take? Was it successfully incorporated by the host organism? These are important, yet difficult, questions to answer. Scientists have no way of knowing where the new gene has gone. They don't know which chromosome it is on. In fact, initially, they don't even know if the gene transfer has worked. So how do they find out whether the gene transfer was successful?

In plants, scientists often transfer two genes at once—the gene of interest and a marker gene. The marker gene lets scientists know whether the transfer occurred. One commonly used marker gene confers resistance to an **antibiotic** known as **kanamycin**. Plant cells that have successfully taken up the gene of interest and the marker gene will be resistant to kanamycin. To determine the success of a gene transfer, the biologist exposes the plant cells to kanamycin. The cells that did not receive the two transferred genes will die. The cells that live must contain the marker gene—and, more importantly, the gene of interest.

To date, there is no reliable way to remove the marker gene for kanamycin resistance from genetically engineered plants. Some critics of genetic engineering worry that people and animals who eat genetically engineered crops may become resistant to kanamycin and related antibiotics. However, since kanamycin is rarely used to treat infections, most experts don't see this as a serious drawback to genetic engineering.

In 1994, the Food and Drug Administration permitted the use of the kanamycin marker gene in new plant varieties after determining that it could not affect the effectiveness of kanamycin in people taking it as an antibiotic. Still, scientists are looking for other possible marker genes.

The Goal of Genetic Engineering

While achieving a successful gene transfer is an important first step in any genetic engineering experiment, the ultimate goal is to create plants and animals with one or more positive characteristics and no negative characteristics. For example, if the goal is to genetically engineer a plant for disease resistance, the disease-resistant plant must still produce a high yield—otherwise its new traits are of no use.

Maintaining valuable characteristics can be a problem if the new genes are somehow interfering with the actions of the plant's other genes. In some cases, initial attempts to introduce new traits result in plants with lower yields or plants that are infertile. Sometimes genetically engineered plants that do well in small laboratory plots perform poorly in large field trials.

Unexpected side effects are not limited to genetic engineering. They can also occur with traditional selective breeding. More knowledge of plant genetics will help scientists control such unwanted effects.

As you can see, it's easier to talk about "gene shuttling" and "gene transfer" than to actually carry it out in the lab. Although the field of recombinant DNA has made great strides in the past 25 years, it still has a long way to go. Nevertheless, its promise has captured the imagination of the public. The government has made it a research priority. Millions of dollars have been spent by private companies eager to capitalize on this wave of the future. The first few crop plants on the market—a tomato, corn, and cotton resistant to insect pests—attracted enormous media attention. The next chapter will look at the first wave of agricultural products developed by recombinant DNA.

-4-
GENETIC ENGINEERING IN PLANTS

The first field trial of a transgenic crop took place in the United States and France in 1986, when tobacco that had been genetically altered with a gene from *A. tumefaciens* was grown.[1] During the next 10 years, more than 3,600 field tests of transgenic crops were conducted by many different companies and universities.[2] Field tests are part of the research and development of a new crop variety. Although many seeds get field-tested, only a few prove to be good enough to be sold commercially.

In 1996, genetically engineered seeds for corn and soybeans became widely available for the first time. In 1997—just 1 year later—10 percent of the United States corn crop and 14 percent of the soybean crop were grown from the genetically engineered seeds.[3] It wasn't long before genetically engineered seeds for **rapeseed**, cotton, potatoes, squash, and tomatoes also became available. Each type of seed offers a characteristic that natural seeds did not. Some protect the plants against insects or disease, while others delay ripening or protect the plants from chemicals used to kill weeds.

Genetically engineered foods have been on supermarket shelves for years, but you probably never realized it. Why not? There are three reasons.

First of all, grain from genetically engineered corn is often mixed with grain from traditionally bred corn to make processed foods. Some of the corn in the cereal you ate for breakfast or the corn chips you ate for lunch was probably grown from genetically engineered seeds. The same is true for soybeans. About 60 percent of all processed foods contain some form of soybeans.[4] (Just look at the labels of your breakfast sausages, salad dressing, and brownie mix. Oil from crushed soybeans is used as vegetable oil and in margarine, chocolate snacks, and other grocery items.)

Secondly, since neither the taste nor the appearance of these crops are altered, the food doesn't seem any different to you.

Finally, since most foods that are genetically engineered or that contain genetically engineered ingredients are not labeled, there is no way for you to know that you are buying or eating them. In most cases, the U.S. government does not require such labeling. Some people believe these foods should be labeled. This hotly debated topic is examined more closely in Chapter 6.

The Food of Our Dreams

Many new strains of grains, fruits, and vegetables created through genetic engineering are expected to come to market in the next decade. Although they will represent many years of work and many dollars spent on scientific research, the ordinary shopper will probably not be aware of the differences. Like the genetically engineered corn and soybeans introduced in 1996, the crops introduced in the near future will not look or taste any different than the plants we eat now. Although researchers are working to use genetic engineering to improve qualities important to consumers—qualities like taste and nutrition—don't expect to see many such products soon. Most industry observers don't anticipate qualities with consumer appeal to appear until 2005.[5]

For now scientists are concentrating on traits that will appeal to the farmer or food processor, rather than the consumer. The new plants will be resistant to insect pests, diseases, or chemicals sprayed on fields to kill weeds. These improvements are invisible to supermarket shoppers, although they may contribute to the variety of foods available or to a food's low cost.

Crop plants that are stronger and produce higher yields are appealing to farmers, but they worry environmentalists. Many crop plants have wild weedy cousins. If the genetically engineered plants were to cross with their wild cousins, the result might be a strain of superweed—one resistant to disease or weed-killers. These superweeds would be extremely difficult to control. Indeed, it is the job of the Environmental Protection Agency to prevent such a scenario. This environmental risk of genetically engineered plants will be examined in greater detail in Chapter 7.

Plants with Insect Resistance

Unprotected plants can be devastated by insect infestations. The European corn borer, for instance, reduces U.S. corn yields by about $1 billion each year. That is why farmers spend millions of dollars on synthetic pesticides to protect their crops from insects. For years, scientists and farmers have known that crop plants genetically engineered to resist insects could save money and increase crop yields.

Organic farmers do not spray synthetic chemicals on their plants. Instead, they rely on a naturally occurring toxic protein taken from a soil bacteria. The bacteria, known as *Bacillus thuringiensis* (Bt), produces a protein that kills caterpillars, beetles, slugs, and other leaf-eating pests. The Bt toxin works by slowly destroying the gut of the insect that ingests it. The insect dies in a few days. This natural toxin does not harm birds, fish, livestock, humans—and even many useful insects—because their digestive systems work differently than those of caterpillars. Organic farmers use the Bt toxin in the form of powders or sprays.

When scientists imagined a genetically engineered crop with resistance against insects, they already knew where to look for the necessary genes. Their target was *B. thuringiensis* genes that coded for toxic proteins. Researchers quickly identified and isolated several Bt genes that signaled the production of toxic proteins. Bt genes were successfully inserted into several crops, including potatoes, cotton, and corn.

In May 1995, the NewLeaf potato—a strain of Russet Burbank potatoes with the Bt gene—received government approval to be sold commercially. This potato, which had been developed by Monsanto, was the first Bt crop to receive this approval. In potatoes, the Bt gene protects against the Colorado potato beetle. Shortly thereafter, Monsanto received government approval for genetically engineered corn seeds sold under the name of YieldGard. In corn, the Bt gene protects against the European corn borer. Monsanto also developed the first cotton crop with Bt protection against the cotton bollworm: BollGard cotton. (Although cotton is most often thought of as a fabric, cottonseed oil is used in food processing.)

In 1996, two additional varieties of corn with the Bt gene received government approval. One variety, called NatureGard, was developed by Mycogen (San Diego, California). Unlike YieldGard, NatureGard has genes known to raise resistance to the European corn borer. Although NatureGard contains several

The tiny European corn borer destroys about $1 billion worth of corn each year in the United States. Several companies have developed genetically engineered varieties of corn that are resistant to the European corn borer.

transferred genes, only one is from a foreign species. Ciba Seeds (Greensboro, North Carolina) introduced its own genetically engineered insect-resistant corn, known as Maximizer.

Thanks to the Bt gene, these genetically altered plants grew leaves that were lethal to hungry insects. With this built-in defense, the plants no longer needed to be sprayed with synthetic chemical pesticides. This benefit is not without its downside, however.

As organic farmers and environmentalists are quick to point out, these new plant strains may actually promote the emergence of caterpillars and beetles that can survive exposure to the Bt toxin. Insects can adapt to chemical pesticides over a period of time. This did not happen with Bt in previous decades when it was used by organic farmers, perhaps because the Bt degraded quickly and insects were exposed for only a short period. But insects munching on plants that contain the Bt toxin in every leaf and stem would receive a much larger dose. This situation could speed the evolution of resistant insects.

Although the development of resistant insects is a major problem and not unique to genetic engineering, critics of the technology say it is especially disastrous in this situation.[6] Not only will the genetically engineered Bt plants become useless, but organic farmers will lose an important natural insecticide.

The best way to address this problem is by creating an arsenal of weapons against leaf-destroying pests, rather than just relying on one defense. Some scientists are doing just that. They are working to identify additional Bt genes that code for insect-killing proteins.

Plants with Herbicide Resistance

The genetically engineered soybean seeds introduced in 1996 have a very desirable characteristic—they are resistant to the most common herbicide used to kill weeds. Weeds steal water and soil nutrients from crop plants, so most farmers use synthetic chemicals to kill them. They spray the herbicides several times each year. The first applications is usually done early in the growing season, before the weeds can take hold. Since herbicides can injure or kill crop plants, farmers must apply them very carefully. If farmers plant crops engineered to resist weed-killing chemicals, they can safely spray herbicides directly on their crops. As a result, the weeds die and the crop plants flourish.

The genetically engineered soybeans that Monsanto introduced in 1996 are resistant to the herbicide glyphosate. Glyphosate, sold under the brand name Roundup, is the best-selling weed killer in the world.[7] In 1996, it accounted for at least 40 percent of Monsanto's profits, according to one analyst.[8] As herbicides go, glyphosate is one of the most environmentally friendly. Because it is broken down quickly by soil microorganisms, little or no toxic byproduct can accumulate in plant or animal tissue. The soybean variety resistant to Roundup was named Roundup Ready.

But here's the wrinkle. At present, plants can be genetically engineered for resistance to only one kind of chemical at a time. Soybeans engineered for resistance to glyphosate, for instance, would be killed by an application of another type of herbicide. The herbicide glufosinate, sold under the brand name

The weed killer glyphosate will not harm these genetically altered soybeans because they contain a bacteria gene that makes them resistant to glyphosate. Glyphosate is sold under the brand name Roundup and this soybean variety is known as Roundup Ready.

Liberty, will kill Roundup Ready soybeans. Unless farmers are planning to use Roundup on their Roundup Ready soybeans, it is pointless to buy the herbicide-resistant crop.

By the end of 1997, Monsanto was also selling rapeseed and cotton resistant to glyphosate, and the company was seeking approval for Roundup Ready corn. Through its subsidiary Calgene, Monsanto also was selling BXN cotton, a variety of cotton resistant to the herbicide bromoxynil. AgrEvo (owned by Hoechst in Frankfurt, Germany) was selling Liberty Link cotton, a variety of cotton resistant to the herbicide Liberty.[9]

The Other Side of the Story

Environmentalists dispute the necessity of creating herbicide-resistant crops. "Why do we want to make it easier to use chemicals on our food crops?" they ask. Critics would like scientists to focus on developing nonchemical methods of weed control. They believe that herbicide-resistant crops will actually increase the use of weed-killers.

One study done in 1996 suggests that environmentalists' fears may be unjustified. It showed that farmers growing herbicide-resistant crops were actually using less herbicide.[10] At the same time, however, the British Agrochemical Association predicted that herbicide sales would benefit from the development of herbicide-resistant crops.

When Roundup Ready soybeans went on the market in 1996, a number of environmental groups voiced their opposition. Greenpeace (Amsterdam, Netherlands) launched several events that focused international attention to the issue. In Iowa, activists sprayed a large pink X on a test field of engineered soybeans on October 10, 1996. In early November, Greenpeace attempted to block shipments of Roundup Ready soybeans in several ports around the world, including New Orleans, Louisiana; Ghent, Belgium; and Hamburg, Germany.

In another widely reported event, an international coalition of health and environmental groups led by Jeremy Rifkin announced on October 6, 1996 that it planned to boycott the manufacturers of ten popular food products unless the companies promised not to use any genetically altered soybeans or corn as ingredients. The products were: Kraft salad dressings,

Coca-Cola, Nestle Crunch, Quaker Oats cornmeal, Green Giant Harvest Burgers, Similac infant formula, Caro corn syrup, McDonald's french fries, Fleischmann's margarine, and Fritos.

The Institute of Food Technologists (Chicago, Illinois) responded to the announcement by issuing a press release declaring that there was no scientific evidence of environmental and health risks associated with genetic engineering. The Grocery Manufacturers of America (Washington, D.C.) publicly announced its support for genetic engineering and observed that the majority of consumers want food products that require fewer pesticides.[11] The companies themselves elected not to respond to the coalition's threat.

In Europe, the Roundup Ready soybeans were the focus of much debate. A lobbying association known as Eurocommerce, which represents about one-third of European retailers, pressed food manufacturers to label products that contained genetically engineered ingredients. The German subsidiaries of Nestle and Unilever, two food companies, announced that they would not buy Roundup Ready soybeans. Nevertheless, the European Union approved sale of the genetically altered soybeans, and no move was made to label products containing Roundup Ready soybeans. Monsanto pointed out that soybeans from many different fields are typically combined before they are sold in bulk. The company argued that it was unrealistic to expect soybean processors to separate out Roundup soybeans for special labeling that was not required by law.

The European response to the soybeans was important because the United States sells about 40 percent of the soybeans it grows to Europe. The European reaction was partly the result of heavy campaigning by Greenpeace and other environmental groups. Fears raised by the outbreak of mad cow disease in Britain in early 1986 also fueled concerns about the safety of the food supply. More cynical observers have argued that European trade groups seized upon the genetic engineering issue simply as an opportunity to protect European markets from foreign products.

As with bovine somatotropin, the genetic engineering of corn and soybeans—the two most important crops in the United States—offered an opportunity for public discussion of farming practices and research goals. And again, debate centered not so much on health and food safety as on environmental and economic issues.

Despite the controversy, genetically engineered crops continue to sell well. Monsanto, the global leader in transgenic crops, planted almost 20 million acres of transgenic crops in 1997—14.1 million acres grew herbicide-resistant crops and 5.4 acres grew Bt crops.[12]

Plants with Disease Resistance

Like weeds and leaf-munching insects, diseases can weaken plants and reduce crop yield. Since many plant viruses are spread by insects, farmers typically fight viral diseases by covering their crops with chemicals designed to kill insects. In addition, new strains of disease-resistant plants have been developed by crossing crop plants with their hardier, wild cousins. Although these new strains gain disease-resistant genes, they often lose other desirable genes and gain undesirable genes in the process. For this reason, new weapons against plant viruses and other diseases are of great interest to farmers.

Recombinant DNA technology gives agricultural scientists new options for developing disease-resistant crop plants. In theory, genetic engineering should allow scientists to transfer only the genes needed for disease resistance, while leaving the undesirable genes behind. Although genetic engineering for disease resistance is not currently being investigated with the same enthusiasm as insect-resistance or herbicide-resistance, some experts believe it will be the next area of genetic engineering to take off. If disease-resistant plants become a reality, there will be less need for chemical pesticides.

The first crop engineered for disease resistance, a strain of yellow crookneck squash, became commercially available in 1995. The Freedom II squash, which is resistant to watermelon mosaic virus 2 and zucchini yellow mosaic virus, was developed by Asgrow Seeds (Kalamazoo, Michigan).*

Since the new squash contained DNA segments obtained from two plant viruses, it needed to be reviewed by the Animal and Plant Health Inspection Service (APHIS), a part of the Environmental Protection Agency. APHIS, which is responsible for preventing the introduction of known or potential plant pests, gave the engineered squash its stamp of approval. In fact, representatives of the agency said the new squash was as safe as traditionally bred virus-resistant squash.[13] Freedom II squash was removed from commercial distribution after the 1995 growing season in order to improve horticultural factors unre-

* The company, now owned by Monsanto, is known today as Asgrow Vegetable Seeds and is based in Saicoy, California.

lated to disease resistance. A new genetically engineered variety—one that is resistant to three viruses—was being prepared by Asgrow in 1997 to take its place.[14] Asgrow Vegetable Seeds has also been developing disease-resistant cucumbers, lettuce, melons, peppers, tomatoes, and watermelons, but these are not yet commercially available.

Plants Engineered for Better Shipping or Processing

Unless you have your own vegetable garden, all of the food you ate today passed through a variety of hands on its journey from the farm to you. Genetic engineering has advantages to offer shippers, food processors, and retailers as well as farmers and consumers. Some qualities can be engineered into fruits and vegetables to make them ship better, with less spoilage and better flavor at the end of their long journey. Retail stores appreciate vegetables that can stay on the shelves longer without rotting. Food processors are always on the lookout for important food ingredients that are cheaper or more pure than the ingredients they currently use.

Fruits that Stay Fresh Longer

The Flavr Savr tomato, the first genetically engineered whole food, was a good example of a food developed to stay fresh longer. By engineering a gene that controlled the softening that comes with ripening, Calgene was able to create a tomato that could ripen on the vine and still be firm enough to ship long distances. This extended freshness was a benefit to the shipper and the retailer, as well as the consumer.

Although the Flavr Savr was taken off the market in 1996, the slow-ripening Endless Summer tomato created by DNA Plant Technology is still available. Other slow-ripening foods in development include bananas, pineapples, strawberries, and raspberries. DNA Plant Technology and Zeneca Plant Science (Wilmington, Delaware) are among the companies engaged in this research.

Potatoes that Absorb Less Oil

French fries are greasy because the potatoes absorb oil when they are deep fried. In the mid-1990s, an experimental potato that absorbs less oil during cooking was developed by Monsanto. These potatoes contain less water and more starch than normal potatoes. They were created by transferring a starch-producing gene from a soil bacterium into the potato. High-starch potatoes cost less to cook into fries, which is a benefit to the processor, and the fries contain less oil, which is a benefit to the consumer. As of 1997, however, the high-starch potato had not yet been commercialized.[15]

Cheaper Food Ingredients

Genetic engineering has been used to create a new source of **laurate**—an ingredient used in chocolate coatings and whipped dessert toppings as well as soaps, detergents, and cosmetics. Laurate occurs naturally in coconut and palm kernel oils. In the mid-

1990s, however, Calgene found a way to transfer a gene from the California bay tree into rapeseed, the plant used to make canola oil. Because rapeseed can be grown in the United States and coconut and palm must be imported, it is less expensive to produce laurate from canola oil. The new variety of rapeseed, known as Laurical, went on the market in 1995.[16]

In addition to Laurical, Calgene is also using genetic engineering to develop varieties of rapeseed with other desirable qualities, such as high levels of sterate and vegetable oil with less saturated fat. Oil with high levels of sterate could take the place of cocoa butter in margarine. This low-fat vegetable oil could be used to make healthier cooking oil and salad dressing.

From the Lab to the Farm to the Supermarket

Taking an experimental crop from the laboratory to the field is an enormous step. Crops that flourish in protected conditions may behave unpredictably in the real world. Overall, the crops introduced in 1996 performed as well as expected. However, Roundup Ready cotton ran into difficulty in some parts of the Mississippi Delta. When farmers there sprayed the crop with Roundup, their plants produced low yields. Monsanto gave the disappointed farmers cash settlements, but refused to admit the company had made any mistakes with the crop. Company officials blamed the problem on freak cold weather and the farmers' lack of familiarity with Roundup Ready cotton. Indeed, Monsanto predicted that the majority of cotton planted in 1999 would be genetically altered.[17]

Although the kinds of genetically engineered improvements described in this chapter are most visible to the people growing, shipping, and processing the crops, biotechnology companies argue that they will also benefit the consumer, perhaps through lower costs or environmental benefits. If the cost of raising crops are lowered, then farmers may pass that savings on to consumers, or so the thinking goes.

Advocates of genetic engineering also argue that if genetically engineered crops reduce the farmer's dependence on chemical herbicides and pesticides, the environment will be better off in the long run. That's good news for everyone. In addition, fruits and vegetables that can be shipped and stored more easily may mean that our supermarkets can be stocked with an even wider variety of foods year-round, a benefit that many shoppers want.

-5-
GENETICALLY ENGINEERED ANIMALS

When genetic engineering was first developed, scientists' imaginations ran wild. They thought about all kinds of incredible genetic modifications. With the successful creation of transgenic mice in 1982, scientists' hopes were raised even higher. "The most obvious application would be the creation of giant pigs, sheep, and cattle, capable of yielding vast quantities of meat and milk," gushed *Time* magazine.[1]

In reality, agricultural work with engineered animals has moved far more slowly and results have been far more modest than originally envisioned. No one is trying to produce giant pigs or cattle. Instead, scientists are focusing on creating leaner meats, more nutritious milk, and higher quality wool. Using the tools of gene transfer to improve disease resistance in farm species is another important goal of the animal scientists.

As of 1997, work with transgenic pigs, sheep, cattle, chickens, and other livestock species was still in the early research stage. Relatively few scientists were working with animals, especially compared to the number investigating transgenic plants. Not until August 1997—4 years after the Flavr Savr tomato could be purchased in the supermarket—was the first conference on transgenic animals in agriculture held. (Sponsored by the University of California, Davis, it was held in Tahoe City, California.) According to James D. Murray, an animal science professor at the University of California, Davis, and the chair of the conference organizing committee, this was first time that enough people around the world were working with transgenic animals to justify holding a meeting.[2]

It will be at least another decade or two before agricultural products made from transgenic farm animals reach the market. Progress is slow, due to a lack of knowledge about animal genes, the expense of working with livestock, and the animals' relatively slow rates of reproduction. In fact, researchers often conduct their experiments on mice and other model species before working with larger animals. This is one way to save time and money, because new techniques can be perfected on mice or rabbits before they are used in cattle and sheep.

Genetic Experiments with Animals in Agriculture

Here are some examples of well-established research projects in the field of transgenic animals in agriculture. Although each research team is working with different livestock species and has different ideas, they share a common goal: to improve methods of genetically engineering animals.

Improving Sheep Wool

Several research groups are working to improve the wool production of merino sheep, the major fine-wool breed in Australia. Wool quality is directly influenced by the presence of certain proteins in the diet. By using genetic engineering to influence the production of those proteins, scientists hope to create sheep that consistently produce wool of the highest quality.

One important amino acid needed for proper wool growth is cysteine. Unfortunately, the quality of sheep feed in Australia varies according to the season. As a result, sheep may not always get the cysteine they need for optimal wool growth.

Merino sheep, an important livestock breed in Australia, are known for their fine wool. Scientists are working to develop genetically engineered sheep that consistently produce high-quality wool.

Scientists working in Blacktown, Australia, at a government laboratory known as CSIRO, Division of Animal Production, hope to solve this problem in an unusual way. The scientists know that certain bacteria are able to make cysteine. By transferring genes from those bacteria into sheep, the team hopes to create transgenic sheep that can actually produce their own cysteine. These transgenic sheep would produce high quality wool all year long.

At the 1997 transgenic animals conference, team leader Kevin Ward announced that the group's experiments had been successful in mice. Although work with sheep had proven difficult, his team had successfully created nine transgenic sheep. Ward and his colleagues were in the process of deciding whether this approach to cysteine deficiency was feasible.

Australian researchers from another lab, the Cooperative Research Centre for Premium Quality Wool at the University of Adelaide, are working with keratin, a protein that is the main component of wool fiber. These researchers hope to increase the strength of wool fibers and, thereby, improve the quality of sheep fleece. Their early efforts have been encouraging.

New and Improved Cow Milk

Cow milk is already an important part of many people's diets. And by changing its protein composition, milk could have even broader appeal. Genetic engineering could decrease the fat content of milk or remove proteins that cause allergic reactions in some people.

Other proposals to change milk are far more ambitious. In theory, it should be possible to create a transgenic cow that produces milk similar to human breast milk, which could replace infant formula. To do this, researchers at the University of California, Davis, hope to create a cow that produces lysozyme—an enzyme found in high quantities in human milk, but not cow milk—in its milk by transferring the human gene for lysozyme into the cow. So far, the group, led by James D. Murray, has been successful in producing transgenic mice that have human lysozyme in their milk. The team is now focused on creating a transgenic cow that does the same thing.

It might also be possible to modify milk so that products such as cheese, ice cream, and yogurt could be manufactured more efficiently. Such milk might have an increased cheese yield, for instance, or have properties that reduce the time required to make cheese. It's even possible that new types of cheese could be created with altered milk from transgenic cows.[3]

Gene Transfer in Chickens and Turkeys

Research to genetically alter chickens and other poultry is being conducted at several centers around the world, including labs at North Carolina State University; Virginia Polytechnic Institute; the University of Guelph; and the United States Department of Agriculture. This work could benefit farmers and consumers tremendously. Improved disease resistance, in particular, would be a welcomed trait.

Unfortunately, genetically engineering poultry is very difficult. Genetic manipulation in animals requires working with a single-celled embryo that can be transferred into a surrogate mother. In poultry, the challenge is to reach the early embryo, introduce new DNA, and then encourage the embryo's growth. This needs to be done when the single-celled egg is in the chicken's oviduct. By the time an egg is laid, it already has about 60,000 cells, so it's too late.

Right now, there is no genetic transfer method that is consistently successful in poultry.[4] Scientists are currently working to develop a method for altering the egg cells of chick embryos. If they are successful, the traits introduced will be passed on to the chick's offspring.

Leaner Pork

The first genetically engineered farm animal was a transgenic pig, developed by the research team at the USDA lab at Beltsville, Maryland, in 1988. The transgenic pig had been created by microinjecting pig embryos with DNA coding for the pig's own growth hormone. The goal was not to create a giant pig, but rather to create an animal with very lean muscle tissue. The experiment did, indeed, result in a pig with lean meat, but the animal also suffered from a variety of ailments, including gastric ulcers, arthritis, and kidney disease.[5] These conditions occurred because the pig produced too much growth hormone. Scientists need to learn more about gene expression in pigs before they can control the amount of growth hormone they produce.

In the years since that experiment, scientists have continued to investigate ways to create transgenic pigs that produce lean meat but are otherwise healthy and normal. Recent efforts by the USDA team, led by Vernon G. Pursel, have focused on manipulating the gene for a protein known as insulin-like growth factor-I (IGF-I), which also plays a role in pig growth. An Australian company, BresaGen Limited, is also working on ways to control the over-expression of growth hormone in transgenic pigs created with growth hormone.

Bigger Fish

The transgenic animal species closest to commercialization is not a livestock animal at all; it is a fish. Several research groups around the world have focused on creating transgenic salmon, carp, and catfish that grow bigger and faster than their ordinary

Catfish that contain additional growth promoting genes grow larger and heavier than normal. The genetically engineered catfish in this photograph was developed at Auburn University in Alabama.

cousins. The transgenic fish have been created, in most cases, by transferring a growth promoting gene taken from rainbow trout. Transgenic catfish have also been created with growth hormone genes from salmon.

Fish are relatively easy to manipulate genetically because their eggs are fertilized outside the body. New genetic material can be easily injected into fish eggs. Unlike work with livestock, there is no need to remove eggs from a female's body and place them into a surrogate mother.[6] The scientific groups at the forefront of transgenic fish research include Fisheries and Oceans Canada, British Columbia; Auburn University in Auburn, Alabama; and the University of Maryland Biotechnology Institute in Baltimore.

Hurdles to Gene Transfer in Animals

Animal engineering has proven quite difficult, and progress is slow. Much of the work so far has concentrated on simple changes, like the introduction of growth hormone genes.[7] One of the main problems in animal research has been finding the right gene to transfer. Our knowledge of animal genetics lags behind that of plant genetics. To make matters even more complicated, most of the traits we value in livestock are the result of the complex interactions of many genes.

In addition, research is slow because scientists do not know how to turn genes "on" and "off," so that proteins are produced only at the correct times. To successfully engineer animals, scientists will need to find better ways to regulate genes and their proteins.

The transgenic pig that suffered from a variety of ailments is one vivid illustration of this hurdle.

The microinjection techniques used by animal scientists (described in Chapter 3) also remain woefully inefficient. Frequently, they don't work. Most of the time, the embryo either fails to integrate the introduced gene or fails to develop and grow properly. Indeed, at the 1997 conference, USDA scientists described how they manipulated 1,207 pig embryos to create just 14 live transgenic piglets. This is obviously a very low success rate.[8]

Other hurdles faced by animal researchers are more mundane. Animal research is very expensive, and it takes years, if not decades, of research to develop transgenic animals that can be used commercially. Animal research moves more slowly than plant work because plants reproduce more quickly and produce many seeds at once. Cattle, by contrast, have a 9-month gestation period and produce only one or two calves at a time. Even mice, which scientists frequently use to develop genetic engineering techniques intended for larger animals, have only ten to twelve litters each year.

Finally, public pressure may influence the direction of animal research in the years to come. Unlike the campaigns mounted against genetically engineered crops, there has been no major opposition to date against the genetic engineering of farm animals. That situation may change, however, as various products get closer to market. Animal research is a controversial subject. So are farming practices that require the confinement of large numbers of animals in crowded conditions. This type of farming is referred to as confinement farming or intensive farming by farmers, and as factory farming by animal rights activists. In the past, activists have often criticized this kind of farming, which is used most frequently with chickens, turkeys, and pigs. If genetic modifications to farm animals, such as disease-resistance or the elimination of aggressiveness, were made so the animals would be better suited for crowding and confinement, it's likely that people would protest.[9]

Pharmaceutical Drugs

Although research into transgenic animals for use in agriculture has moved rather slowly, another area of transgenic animal research has made steady strides forward. We're accustomed to thinking of livestock animals as producers of meat, milk, or wool. However some scientists are working to create animals that produce pharmaceutical drugs rather than improved agricultural products. Their goal is to engineer goats or cows or sheep that produce specific proteins in their milk that have value as a human or animal drug.

Research that focuses on pharmaceutical products requires relatively few changes in the animal and, at the same time, promises big financial payoffs. By contrast, agricultural products, like milk and meat, are sold relatively cheaply. Large quantities of those products must be sold before the farmer can earn a significant amount.

Raising transgenic livestock that produce pharmaceutical products is called, rather playfully, **pharming**, and the animals that express the new proteins are called **bioreactors**. The animals have also been described as "living factories."[10]

PPL Therapeutics, which oversees farms in Roslin, Scotland; Blacksburg, Virginia; and Whakaru, New Zealand, is a leader in this field. The company successfully used a human gene to create a transgenic sheep that produces a protein known as alpha-1-antitrypsin (AAT) in its milk. The protein was developed for the treatment of lung disorders, including cystic fibrosis.[11] In 1997, the drug was being tested in clinical trials.

The genetic engineering techniques used with animals are the same whether the goal is new pharmaceutical products or new agricultural products. As a result, there is a great deal of research overlap. This book, however, focuses primarily on the genetic engineering of animals for agricultural traits.

What about Cloning?

PPL Therapeutics captured the world's attention in February 1997 when its research arm, Roslin Institute, announced that it had successfully created a clone—an exact replica—of an adult sheep. The clone, named Dolly, was created from an egg cell specially prepared in the Institute's laboratory near Edinburgh, Scotland. The egg cell had been incubated in the lab as a tiny embryo for 6 days before being transferred into the uterus of a surrogate mother sheep. About 5 months later, on July 5, 1996, Dolly was born. The Scottish team, headed by Ian Wilmut, waited to publicize its success until the experiment was described in the February 27, 1997 issue of the scientific journal *Nature*.[12]

The egg that led to Dolly's birth was created with cellular material from two sheep. Mammary cells

A sheep named Dolly was the world's first clone of an adult mammal. Scientists at the Roslin Institute in Edinburgh, Scotland, created Dolly from the mammary cells of a 6-year-old ewe.

were scraped from the udder of one sheep, a 6-year-old Finn Dorset ewe. These cells were kept alive in a test tube with a special liquid culture that prevented them from dividing. At the same time, an egg cell was removed from another sheep and its nucleus was extracted, so that the egg no longer contained any DNA. Next, a mammary cell was inserted into the egg. When an electrical charge was applied to the egg, it accepted the new nucleus. The egg was tricked into believing it had been fertilized. It began dividing normally and, after 6 days, was transferred into a surrogate mother. When Dolly was born, she was the identical twin of the Finn Dorset ewe, although 6 years younger, of course. Since the birth of Dolly, other cloned animals have been born, including calves.[13]

Dolly's birth marked a tremendous achievement in animal genetics research. Although scientists have been able to split embryos into identical twins for several years, this was the first time a clone had been created from the cell of an adult animal. In theory, this meant that a superior animal, one known for exceptional milk or wool or meat, could spawn an entire herd of identical specimens. The superior animal could be one that occurred naturally, or even one that had been created through genetic engineering.

In reality, however, the scientific process that led to the creation of Dolly suffered from the same drawbacks that haunt other animal genetics researchers. It was inefficient and unreliable. The experiment that yielded one success, namely Dolly, also had a great many failures. The Scottish team attempted the process 277 times. Only 30 eggs divided successfully. Of those, 29 were suitable for transfer into a surrogate mother, and only one surrogate gave birth to a live lamb.

Still, the Dolly success paved the way for other genetics that may have little to do with cloning. In an interview with the *New York Times*, Ian Wilmut noted that, "The overall aim is actually not, primarily, to make copies. It's to make precise genetic changes in cells."[14]

Headlines around the world trumpeted the story of Dolly, and rightly so. The cloning of an adult animal caused an enormous shift in the way we think about ourselves and our unique natures. "In much the way that the Wright brothers at Kitty Hawk freed humanity of a restriction once considered eternal," wrote the *New York Times* reporters, "human existence suddenly seems to have taken on a dramatic new dimension."[15] But, just as it was a long way from the Wright brothers' flight experiments to commercial air travel, so will it be a long way from the Dolly experiment to practical benefits of cloning in agriculture.

-6-
GOVERNMENT REGULATION AND LABELING

In the United States, genetically engineered fruits, vegetables, and food ingredients are regulated by the government, just like any other food. If a new product contains material already found in the food supply, then it is regarded as safe and the company that developed does not need special permission to put it on the market. In other words, a transgenic catfish containing a trout gene would be considered safe to eat because it is already well-known that trout is harmless to humans. Nor does the government require genetically modified fruits, vegetables, or food ingredients to be labeled. As a result, you have no way of knowing whether your pizza sauce was made with engineered tomatoes or whether your corn-on-the-cob carries the Bt gene. That's as it should be, the government has declared, because food safety should focus on the product rather than on the process that created it.

Not everybody is happy with this policy. A number of activist groups, including the Pure Food Campaign, the Environmental Defense Fund, and the Union for Concerned Scientists (Washington, D.C.), have opposed the government's policies, particularly the labeling decision. Why is the decision to label—or not to label—such a heated one? To appreciate this ongoing debate, it's important to understand how food is regulated in the United States.

How Is Food Safety Regulated in the U.S.?

In the United States, the USDA and FDA are responsible for food safety. The USDA inspects and grades meat, poultry, and milk. The FDA develops standards for food safety, inspects food plants, and recalls unsafe or contaminated foods. But it rarely gets involved when a new food is offered for sale. Every year, 10,000 to 20,000 new food products are introduced, from cereals to low-fat dinners to desserts. (The typical supermarket contains more than 30,000 products.[1]) Almost all of these new food products can be sold without first contacting the FDA. This is because the company that makes them can guarantee that the product contains only ingredients with a history of safe use in food.

The only time the law requires testing of a new food is when it contains an additive that is not known and, therefore, not generally regarded as safe. ("Generally regarded as safe," or GRAS, is actually the technical term used.) Artificial sweeteners and food colors are examples of unfamiliar food additives. In that instance, the company must conduct tests showing the safety of the additive and receive FDA approval before it is permitted to sell the new product.

This system of evaluating new foods had been in place for more than 50 years when the first transgenic fruits and vegetables were being developed in the 1980s. The FDA needed to make a decision regarding the regulation of genetically engineered foods.

Activist groups wary of the new technology recommended that the FDA treat the expression of transferred genetic material as a food additive.[2] The Environmental Defense Fund also recommended that manufacturers of genetically engineered food should be required to notify the FDA of the composition of such foods 3 months prior to sale.

On the other side of the debate were groups supported by the food industry, including the International Food Information Council (Washington, D.C.) and the Biotechnology Industry Organization (Washington, D.C.). These organizations argued that the products of genetically altered crops should be judged on their individual safety and nutrition, rather than on the methods used to produce them. They believed that the engineered crops should be regulated in the same way as other foods.[3]

It was during this period, as the FDA was gathering information with which to make its decision, that Calgene voluntarily sought FDA approval for the Flavr Savr tomato. The Flavr Savr was the first genetically engineered whole food to reach the market. FDA review of the tomato was not required, as no guidelines had yet been established regulating engineered food. Yet to encourage public confidence in its product, Calgene sought FDA acceptance of its product.

On May 29, 1992, the FDA issued guidelines describing how it would regulate genetically engineered crops.[4] The guidelines stated that new genes did not qualify as food additives. Just because the gene had been placed there through recombinant DNA techniques did not automatically make it a food additive. Rather, the guidelines stated, the focus should be on whether the protein expressed by the new gene was familiar and could be generally regarded as safe. Since most genetically engineered crops relied on genes that were already present in other food crops, the FDA concluded that, in most cases, companies would not be required to notify the FDA before they began selling genetically engineered foods made from plants.

Of course, new proteins expressed by genes from unfamiliar sources would require consultation with the FDA. Although its review of the Flavr Savr tomato occurred before the new guidelines were issued, the FDA treated the protein produced by the kanamycin-resistant gene as a food additive. (Kanamycin resistance, as described in Chapter 3, is used as a marker gene during the research and development of genetically engineering foods.) Calgene conducted a variety of tests demonstrating the safety of the protein for human consumption. After evaluating Calgene's tests, the FDA approved the use of the new protein as a food additive. The FDA also concluded that the Flavr Savr was not significantly different from other tomatoes.

The 1992 FDA guidelines made it clear that the FDA considered genetic engineering of crops an extension of traditional plant breeding techniques. The FDA was not going to evaluate every food made from transgenic crops. This decision was seen as a major victory for the food industry.

Guarding against Allergic and Other Toxic Reactions

In those same 1992 guidelines, the FDA stated that labels were not required on genetically engineered food unless the food was likely to cause reactions in allergic individuals or the engineering process had significantly changed the food's nutritional content. It would be the company's responsibility to determine whether a new food fell into either of those categories. If they did, the FDA would require a label.

Certainly the biggest issue, by far, is the allergy question. Peanuts and other nuts, fish, milk, wheat, and shellfish are known to cause reactions in certain people. These reactions can cause mild discomfort, severe shock, or even death. People with food allergies are accustomed to avoiding the foods that make them sick. But if a gene from one of those foods was transferred to another food, like a banana, it would be impossible for them to avoid it. A label on the transgenic banana would be very important.

It is unlikely that every gene in, say, a peanut produces an allergenic protein. Yet the FDA is cautious. The agency acts under the assumption that any gene taken from a food that is known to cause allergic reactions is likely to cause a reaction when it is transferred into a new food. Therefore, any product containing a gene from an allergenic food would be subject to labeling requirements.

Unfortunately, the proteins responsible for allergic reactions are poorly understood. In an experiment followed closely by the scientific community in the early 1990s, a large seed company named Pioneer

Hi-Bred transferred a gene from the Brazil nut into soybeans. The company was hoping to create a soybean with extra protein to use in animal feed. Pioneer Hi-Bred checked the new soybean for allergens, as the 1992 FDA guidelines instructed. When tests showed that the transgenic soybean caused an allergic reaction, Pioneer Hi-Bred and the FDA together decided to stop the project because the soybeans posed a risk to allergy-sensitive individuals. (Although the company's goal was to develop an improved animal feed, it would have been impossible to guarantee that none of the transgenic soybeans ever entered the human food supply.[5])

The FDA recognizes that even with labeling, protecting allergic people from eating genetically engineered food that contains allergenic proteins could be extremely difficult. People often eat food that they don't buy or prepare themselves. For this reason, the FDA prevents the marketing of genetically engineered food that is likely to produce serious reactions in allergic individuals.

Moreover, the FDA requires a label if a foreign gene significantly changes the composition of a food. Tomatoes, for instance, are an important source of vitamin C. If a variety of genetically engineered tomatoes was known to contain significantly less—or more—vitamin C, then it would have to be labeled. Similarly, if the concentration of naturally occurring toxins in a new food were increased by genetic engineering, this food would also need a label. (Many foods, including tomatoes, potatoes, peppers, and lima beans, contain naturally occurring toxins, but at levels harmless to humans.[6])

Although it seems unlikely that engineering for one trait—such as longer shelf life—could affect another trait—such as vitamin or toxin levels—it could happen. And, in fact, it has happened during traditional plant breeding. In the late 1960s, long before genetic manipulation of foods in the laboratory, researchers at the USDA introduced the Lenape potato. It was bred for its high solids content, a trait important to potato chip manufacturers. Two years later, the Lenape potato was withdrawn from the market after scientists realized that it contains high levels of a toxic substance known as solanine.[7]

In another example, some tomato varieties bred for mechanical harvesting (so-called square tomatoes) were found to have 15 percent less vitamin C than other varieties. Somehow selecting for the genes for square shape resulted in the loss of genes for vitamin C production.[8] These two examples demonstrate how even a process as familiar as traditional plant breeding can have unexpected results.

Labeling Controversy Continues

Despite these exceptions to the FDA's no-labeling policy, some people are still dissatisfied with the policy. According to a national survey of 1,004 U.S. adults taken in March 1997, 78 percent initially supported the FDA policy. However, after being presented with the position of some critics, support dropped to 57 percent.[9] Another survey of American adults showed that 90 percent wanted labeling. This survey was sponsored by Novartis, the gigantic multinational company created through a merger of the Swiss companies Ciba-Geigy and Sandoz. In February 1997, Novartis announced that it supported labeling of genetically engineered foods based on the results of this survey.[10]

Almost all other companies have resisted labeling, however, because the food industry is concerned that informative labels would be read by shoppers as warnings. Labeling would also be costly, they argue. Most likely, that expense would be passed on to the consumer.

Labeling also poses some difficult questions. It's one thing to slap a sticker on a transgenic tomato or banana. But if those tomatoes are used to make sauce, should the tomato sauce also be labeled? What if the sauce is spread on a pizza? Should the pizza be labeled? If chickens are fed genetically altered corn, should their meat be labeled? What if their meat is used in soup? Should the soup be labeled too? Engineered soybeans and corn are routinely processed into hundreds of different kinds of foods. Should all those products be labeled? Obviously, our food production system is complicated. This makes the implications of requiring labels immense.

The Special Case of Bovine Growth Hormone

The issue of labeling was particularly heated in regard to bovine growth hormone (bovine somatotropin). When Monsanto's genetically engineered bovine growth hormone, Posilac, was approved for use in 1993, several food companies, including Ben & Jerry's, worked hard to publicize the fact that their products were made only from cows that had not received injections of recombinant bovine somatotropin (rBST).[11]

Yet their first attempts to label their products were thwarted. In response to their labels, the FDA promptly issued guidelines warning against such labels since all milk contains natural bovine somatotropin. Even the phrase "from cows not treated with rBST" was judged to be misleading since it implied that such milk was safer than other milk.[12] Four states—Illinois, Hawaii, Nevada, and Oklahoma—soon passed laws that forbid the placement of antihormone labels on dairy products. These laws effectively stopped anti-rBST labeling because it was impractical for companies to label their products differently for different states.

In May 1996, Ben & Jerry's filed suit in Illinois federal court to receive permission to put a label on its products. The suit was joined by several other natural food companies, including Whole Foods Market, which is based in Austin, Texas. Whole Foods Market owns Fresh Fields, a national chain of supermarkets. The companies charged that the prohibition on labeling violated their First Amendment right to inform their customers of their products' contents. In August 1997, a settlement was announced between the state of Illinois and the food companies. Under the settlement, makers of ice cream, yogurt, and other dairy products are now permitted to label their products with the following message:

We oppose recombinant bovine growth hormone. The family farmers who supply our milk and cream pledge not to treat their cows with rBGH. The FDA has said no significant difference has been shown and no test can now distinguish between milk from rBGH treated and untreated cows.[13]

Labeling controversies like these illustrate the public's uneasiness with genetically engineered foods. Despite government assurances that such foods are safe, polls indicate that the majority of people want information—labels—so that they can make their own decisions about what they are eating. Although food safety is assured by the FDA, food safety is not the only criterion people use to evaluate the food they eat. The next chapter examines other factors people consider when they are trying to make up their minds about genetically engineered food.

-7-
OBJECTIONS TO GENETICALLY ENGINEERED FOODS

Genetically engineered foods are something the world has never seen before. Like all new technologies, genetic engineering has both potential benefits and potential drawbacks. People who support genetic engineering in agriculture believe that the advantages will outweigh any disadvantages. Other people believe just the opposite.

Much of the controversy over genetically engineered foods has focused on the risk to the environment. Could the introduction of transgenic crops somehow lead to a new variety of superweeds? Will Bt crops cause the rise of a generation of Bt-resistant insect pests? Unfortunately, risk—especially long-term risk—is difficult to measure.

Economic, social, and philosophical concerns also influence the acceptance of genetically engineered foods. For many people, such concerns are as important as—or even more important than—health and safety issues. These people want to know whether transgenic crops will force small family farms out of business. Or they may feel it is morally wrong to transfer genes from one species into another.

Opposition to genetically engineered food varies in different parts of the world. It has been very strong in some parts of Europe. The European Union has proposed strict labeling. Austria and Luxembourg have banned genetically engineered food.[1] Polls have shown that only 22 percent of people in Austria and 30 percent of people in Germany are willing to buy genetically engineered produce. By contrast, 74 percent of the people surveyed in Canada and 73 percent of the people surveyed in the United States are willing to buy genetically engineered fruits and vegetables.[2]

Despite this acceptance among the U. S. public, a number of organizations have strongly opposed the genetic manipulation of food crops. The best-known of these are the National Wildlife Federation, the Environmental Defense Fund, the Union of Concerned Scientists, Greenpeace, and the Foundation on Economic Trends. Although these groups are different in many ways, they share a similar skepticism regarding genetic engineering and agriculture. In general, they would like to see genetically engineered crops more strictly regulated and consumer products labeled. Through their activism—including rallies, press conferences, brochures, and World Wide Web pages on the Internet—these groups work to inform and influence the public. Interested voters are encouraged to express their concerns by writing their representatives in Congress or policy makers at the Food and Drug Administration.

More rarely, citizens are urged to boycott genetically engineered foods. One of the first—and certainly the most publicized—boycotts occurred in

1992, shortly after the FDA announced its guidelines for genetically engineered food. Jeremy Rifkin prompted a boycott of genetically engineered food among restaurant chefs. More than 1,500 restaurants nationwide, including some of the country's most prestigious eateries, joined the boycott. Although the boycott did draw attention to the arrival of genetically engineered foods, it lasted less than 2 years.

On the other side of the debate are various food industry and biotechnology groups, like the Institute of Food Technologists, the International Food Information Council, and the Biotechnology Industry Organization. These groups support the genetic manipulation of food crops. One of the biggest supporters of research in agricultural biotechnology has been the U.S. government. Through millions of dollars in research grants, the government has actively encouraged the research and development of genetically manipulated crops. The government sees this new technology as a way to increase agricultural productivity and to stay competitive in the world market. Certainly the government is sending a clear message that it believes the potential good outweighs any possible harm.

At one time, the government's endorsement of a new technology would have been reassuring to the majority of U.S. citizens. In the past, technology was considered unquestionably good, a force that could make our lives better, our purses fatter, and our nation stronger. This kind of thinking was common in the years following World War II.

Most Americans no longer have this attitude. We have seen the horrors that sometimes come with technological developments. In Europe, the drug thalidomide caused devastating birth defects in the 1960s.

The demise of the bald eagle and other wildlife species has been linked to the use of DDT, a pesticide. In December 1984, a Union Carbide factory in Bhopal, India, exploded, releasing toxic gas that killed up to 2,500 people. In April 1986, a nuclear power plant failed in Chernobyl, in the Ukraine. Major chemical and oil spills have occurred around the globe and filled our television sets with images of dead birds, animals, and fish. We now know that technology carries both promise and peril, and that risk is often unpredictable and difficult to contain.

Public trust in the government is also failing. Controversy over the Vietnam War, political scandals like Watergate, and more recent disclosures of wrongdoing have undermined public confidence in the government. Rather than blindly trusting the government, people are now evaluating new technology for themselves. They are taking responsibility for their own health and well-being.

Combine these two trends with something as fundamental as food and as unfamiliar as gene transfer, and the show of public concern is predictable. Genetically engineered foods? Sounds spooky. The government says genetic engineering is safe? Sounds dubious.

Some people are easily swayed by emotional arguments against genetically engineered foods. After all, it certainly sounds unappealing to hear that your food contains a bacterium gene. It's frightening to hear genetically engineered food called "Frankenfood."

Knowing a little bit about the science behind genetic engineering helps people evaluate the many arguments they are likely to hear. One study showed that after attending a 20-minute presentation on genetic engineering in agriculture, people were more likely to recognize that the new technology has potential benefits, as well as risks. Some people learned for the first time that the government was responsible for food safety and human health. Access to accurate scientific information made people look more favorably upon genetically engineered crops.[3]

Not all concerns can be addressed by further education, however. Reasonable, knowledgeable, and intelligent people can be found on both sides of the debate over genetically engineered food. This reflects a basic disagreement over principles, values, and future risks and benefits.

Earlier chapters in this book examined specific concerns related to particular genetically engineered crops. This chapter will look at more general objections, ones that apply to the new technology as a whole, rather than a specific product.

Environmental Concerns

Crop plants that have been engineered to be stronger, fitter, and better able to withstand the onslaught of disease and insects are appealing to farmers. But unfortunately, there is a significant drawback to creating such plants. All crop plants have wild cousins that are weeds—plants that fail to produce useful fruit or fiber, yet grow quickly and easily. What would happen if a genetically engineered crop and its wild cousins crossed? What if a weed with a genetically manipulated gene that made it resistant to insects or disease or weed-killer were created? What if engineered crop plants themselves became weeds?

Ordinarily, crop plants are delicate and will die without proper watering, weeding, and fertilizers. Some people fear that scientists might be able to develop a crop plant that resists disease or insects so well that it spreads into the wild and threatens the ecology of that region. Imagine: corn taking over forests and meadows or an explosion of potatoes in your neighborhood!

In North America, broccoli, cauliflower, rapeseed, and other members of the Brassica family of plants have many wild relatives. For these plants, the problem of new genes passing from crops into weeds is a real issue. Indeed, the transfer of genes from ordinary rapeseed into its weedy relatives has been observed and documented. Soybeans and squash also have wild cousins. In 1993, prior to the introduction of virus-resistant squash, the National Wildlife Federation voiced concern that cross-pollination between the squash and the Texas gourd, a weedy wild relative, was likely and might increase the weediness of the gourd.

Many crops grown in North America have no wild cousins, so they pose no threat of passing their new genes to weeds. But the risk of crops crossing with wild relatives is very real in other parts of the world. Corn has wild relatives in Mexico and South America, for instance, and tomatoes have wild relatives in South America. Rice, which is grown in China and India, also has weedy wild cousins.

How likely is it for a new gene—or any gene—to move from crop plants into the weed population? How might the strengthened weeds affect the environment? Unfortunately, these are very difficult questions to answer. Scientists can design experiments that measure the likelihood of a particular event happening in one growing season. They can gauge what the immediate results of that event may be. But it's extremely difficult to measure long-term risk or predict how an entire ecosystem may be affected by a change in one small population. Our understanding of ecology and ecosystems is just not that sophisticated.

Despite the difficulties in predicting the future of a particular ecosystem, past examples of havoc caused by the introduction of a foreign species abound. Kudzu, a vine native to Asia, became a plant pest in the southern U.S. after it was introduced in the late 1800s, for example. Dutch elm disease, African bees, gypsy moths, and dandelions are other nonnative species that destroyed native ecosystems in the United States. None of these species are genetically engineered, of course, but the concern is that a superweed created through a cross between a weed and a transgenic crop could act the same way.

Preventing these disasters is the responsibility of the Animal and Plant Health Inspection Service. APHIS works closely with companies involved in the research and development of genetically engineered crops to make sure that no plant pests are introduced into the environment. Beginning in 1986, when the first transgenic crop was field tested, APHIS required field testing permits for such crops. APHIS reviews the genetic background of each crop and reviews the company's plans for the test. If the permit is approved, APHIS establishes the rules under which the test can be conducted.

In more recent years, APHIS has decided that six genetically engineered crops—corn, cotton, potato, soybean, tobacco and tomato—are so well-understood that they don't require prior approval before field testing. (Tobacco is often used as a model plant in genetic experiments. No transgenic tobacco is commercially sold.) This knowledge is based upon field tests conducted on these crops between 1986 and 1993. APHIS believes that tests of these crops pose no threat to the environment. Companies wishing to field test crops other than these six, however, are still obligated to apply for a permit.

Some transgenic crops are also regulated by the Environmental Protection Agency. Among its many duties, the EPA is responsible for regulating the manufacture and use of all pesticides. For this reason, the EPA reviews applications for field test permits for crop plants engineered to resist herbicides or viruses. The agency also reviews applications for pesticide-producing crops, like Bt corn.

Environmental groups have argued that the government regulations need to be stricter. The government, in turn, has stated that the regulations are adequate. The debate pivots on disagreement over how easily unwanted consequences can be prevented or controlled. Since the end of 1996, this debate has eased somewhat. The risks presented by most genetically modified plants appear to be smaller than originally feared. Still, both environmental groups and APHIS are sensitive to the risk that certain manipulated genes might pose in certain environments.

Philosophical Concerns

For many people, gene transfer raises the uneasy sense that we are tampering with life itself. Genetic engineers have been accused of "playing God." As early as 1976, in an issue of *Science*, Nobel Prize-winner Erwin Chargoff questioned whether science has the right "to counteract, irreversibly, the evolutionary wisdom of millions of years" by transferring genes from one species into another.[4] On its World Wide Web page, Greenpeace warns against "dabbling with genes to produce unnatural living plants, and animals." In a 1991 press release, Jeremy Rifkin stated that the proliferation of transgenic species "could mean the end of the natural world as we currently know it."[5] Christine M. Bruhn, director of the Center for Consumer Research at the University of California, Davis, notes that some people invoke a religious perspective, arguing that God gave humanity free reign to control and conquer the natural world.[6]

Of course, not all genetic engineering involves the transfer of genes between species. The Flavr Savr tomato, for example, was created by altering one of the tomato's own genes. Some people may find that kind of manipulation acceptable. Others may be comfortable only with gene transfer between plant species. In fact, surveys have shown that people are more willing to accept gene transfer in plants than in animals, and that people are most uncomfortable with the transfer of human genes into plants and animals. There is a general feeling that the border between humankind and the rest of the animal world must be strongly maintained. Underlying this sentiment is the squeamish feeling that human qualities will somehow accompany the transfer of human DNA into a cow or sheep.

Vegetarians and certain religious orders are also concerned about the transfer of animal genes into the plants they eat. Vegetarians, of course, avoid eating meat. Some religious groups are forbidden to eat certain kinds of animals. Orthodox Jews, for example, don't eat pork or shellfish. Would an animal gene inserted into a fruit make that fruit unacceptable to a vegetarian? Would the presence of a pig gene in a vegetable make it off-limits to an Orthodox Jew? The Kosher Union does not consider genetic engineering unacceptable, but individual rabbis may decide differently.[7]

The FDA has responded to these philosophical arguments by pointing out that plants and animals, including humans, share many genes. In 1993, James H. Maryanski, biotechnology coordinator for the FDA, observed, "There is a gene that occurs in rice that also occurs in the human brain. Vegetarians would not avoid rice because of that." Maryanski also stated that the FDA believes that genetically modified foods do not violate any ethical or religious principles.[8]

And what of the argument that gene transfer is just "unnatural"? Does this mean that science does not have the right to alter what is found in nature? If this were true, surgery, hearing aids, and eyeglasses would also be objectionable. A destructive hurricane is "natural" but that doesn't make it good. Arguments that claim that natural is synonymous with good are often shortsighted and overly simplistic.

Objections to genetically engineered food that are based in religious or philosophical beliefs are legitimate. They may not be compelling enough to influence government policy, however, and the temptation then becomes to cloak those beliefs as concern over human health and safety.[9] This is unfortunate, since it becomes more difficult to differentiate scientific fact from personal conviction.

Protecting the Family Farm

In the early 1990s, as the potential impact of recombinant DNA on agriculture became clear, supporters of the family farm viewed the new technology with suspicion. What kind of small farmer would it help? Who might it hurt? Would the introduction of genetically engineered crops hasten the trend toward fewer, larger farms?

Family farms have always had a hold on the American imagination. The small farm that is owned and worked by a single family has long been viewed as a symbol of independence and self-reliance. Working in harmony with nature and each other, the family members tended their chores, their crops, and their livestock, and were able to make an honest living. In the writings of many of our country's founders, especially Thomas Jefferson, family farms were thought to be good for building moral character and important for the survival of democracy.[10]

For most of history, equipment and farming practices were well-suited to the family-sized farm. But advances in mechanization in the twentieth century made it possible to run a very large farm efficiently and with relatively few workers. In 1950, the average farm was about 200 acres (81 hectares). In 1983, it was 450 acres (182 ha). In the 1930s, farmers comprised 25 percent of the population. By the 1990s, they made up less than 3 percent of the population.

Today, almost all farms are still owned by families. (Only 3 percent are organized as corporations, and many of the corporations are family owned.) But a family-owned farm is not necessarily a family-sized farm. Indeed, the trend in farming is toward larger

Farmers worked small parcels of land with animals and basic equipment for many centuries. Not until the twentieth century did mechanization make it possible for relatively few workers to farm many acres of land.

and larger farms that are run by professional managers and hired workers. In 1988, for instance, farms with sales in excess of $250,000 made up only 4.9 percent of all farms. But that tiny 4.9 percent produced 55 percent of all farm cash receipts.[11]

In recent years, the small farmer has been dealt a number of blows. One of the worst came in the 1980s, when a financial crisis forced many small farmers out of business. The widespread foreclosure of farms, especially in the Midwest, sparked sympathy and support from the public who recognized that a way of life was passing. Although the land itself might continue to support crops or livestock, it would become part of a larger farm. As farm size increased, the number of farmers decreased. Many families who had worked small farms for generations were forced to sell their property.

Nostalgia was not the only reason to be disturbed by these events. In theory, it's easier for an industry to raise prices and limit consumer choices when only a few owners are in control. For this reason, some people believed it was better to have many small farms than a few large ones.

Not everyone lamented the loss of so many small farms, however. Some agricultural economists believed that only inefficient producers were forced out of business. The farms that remained were necessarily those with the best management and farming practices, they argued. In this Darwinian view, the economic crisis of the 1980s served to keep the farming industry fit and competitive.

During this period of upheaval, it's no wonder that crops created through recombinant DNA techniques were viewed suspiciously. For the most part, however, genetically engineered seeds seem to benefit large and small farms equally. Seeds are simple, familiar, and low-tech. Unlike new equipment, which requires a large investment of money and training, no enormous costs or specialized skills are required.

Even if genetically engineered products were shown to adversely affect small farms, that's no reason for the government to withdraw its support of the new technology. Historically, the government has never considered social or economic factors when evaluating a new product. Yet, the government also works to support the stability of rural communities. As a result, some policy makers have argued that the government should withhold funding and approval to any genetically engineered products that could hurt small farmers.

Anticorporate Argument

Genetic engineering changed the face of agricultural research. Historically, new seed varieties in the United States were developed by agricultural colleges and government labs. Research into hybrid corn led to the founding of private seed companies, like Pioneer Hi-Bred, which were devoted to the sale of hybrid corn. But not until the rise of genetic engineering did enormous multinational companies show much interest in the seed business. Such companies had been known for their chemicals, pharmaceuticals, and many other products—but not seeds. Monsanto, for instance, was founded in 1901 as Monsanto Chemical Works. Its first products included aspirin and saccharine. The involvement of these kinds of companies in agriculture research was a new phenomenon that created a new set of concerns.

A few decades ago, a farmer could expect to buy fertilizer, pesticide, and seeds from three different companies. With the entrance of the large chemical companies into the seed business, farmers can now buy all they need from just one company. Some fear that this could lead to monopolies and increased prices. Furthermore, highly publicized lay-offs in recent years have eroded public confidence in large corporations. That lack of confidence has prompted some people to wonder whether the large companies have their best interests at heart. Will these companies adequately address questions related to public health and safety? Or will the press for profits prompt them to rush new products to the market without adequate testing? Mistrust of big business has added yet another hurdle to public acceptance for genetically engineered foods.

Commercial interest in genetic engineering has also changed the way agricultural research is conducted. Historically, agricultural research meant traditional plant breeding, and much of the work was done at state-funded universities that had been specifically established to offer programs in agriculture. The university scientists saw themselves as public servants supported by taxpayers. Through university extension services, the scientists offered practical advice to farmers. New seed varieties were frequently made available to farmers with no thought of turning a profit.

With the rise of genetic engineering, many profit-seeking companies, both large and small, were eager to get involved and stake out their interests. One popular way to do this was to fund university researchers in exchange for gaining some control over their research results. For example, in exchange for receiving research money from a particular company, a university scientist might agree to release experiment results only to that company and to allow only that company to conduct large-scale field tests on the plants. If all went well, the company would eventually take responsibility for growing, advertising, and marketing the new variety. Profits from the sale of the vegetable or seed would go to the company, although the university scientist might share in a percentage of the profits.

Does this sound like a situation where everybody wins? To many people it did, especially since it came at a time when state governments had less money to give to state universities. Indeed, the administrations of both President Ronald Reagan and President George Bush encouraged universities and corporations to work together and to carry more laboratory research through to commercial development. This was known as "technology transfer." But for the university scientist, this new relationship meant serving two masters: the public and the corporation. Unfortunately, the two often have competing demands. Freely sharing research results, for instance, advances knowledge. This benefits the public. But companies often don't want new techniques or new findings shared until they can acquire a patent for the research. In some cases, they don't ever want the research shared. They want to keep it as a trade secret instead.

Could state-funded universities enter into corporate partnerships and still serve the public good? Or would their advice and research now be slanted—even unintentionally—toward the company that gave the most research money? This became the critical question. To some people, genetically engineered products had led to a situation that was good for neither the small farmer nor the rural economy. For an agricultural school to accept corporate dollars to fund such research seemed a betrayal of trust.

Sustainable Agriculture

Where is agriculture headed? For decades, agriculture focused on one goal: increased yield per acre. Intensive farming practices that depended upon pesticides, weed-killers, and increased mechanization were developed to meet that aim. Corn yield, for instance, went from 24 bushels per acre (342 liters per hectare) in 1935 to about 130 bushels per acre (1,854 L/ha) today. But some farming practices that increase yield can result in contaminated groundwater, soil erosion, and other damage to the environment. Faced with numerous examples of ecological disaster, there is a growing sense that we need to be responsible stewards of the natural world, including the land we farm.

Sustainable agriculture is the term used to describe agricultural practices intended to sustain the land for future generations. Sustainable agriculture is meant to be ecologically sound, as well as profitable. Farmers who practice sustainable agriculture adopt farming practices that protect soil and water quality. These men and women tend to think of the farm as an ecosystem, as well as a business.

One of the most obvious characteristics of sustainable agriculture is its rejection of chemical pesticides and herbicides. Instead of chemicals, farmers work to control disease, weeds, and insects by rotating the crops they plant. By contrast, commercial farmers tend to plant the same crops year after year. This encourages large populations of insects to take hold. The farmers typically respond with applications of chemical pesticides. By rotating crops, pest populations are less likely to gain a stronghold. Sustainable agriculture also encourages the use of natural pesticides, like Bt, and scouting for insect pests by hand.[12]

Sustainable agriculture depends upon shoppers as well as farmers. Fruits and vegetables grown without chemical pesticides are often not as perfect in appearance as produce grown by conventional means. Shoppers who support sustainable agriculture buy them anyway. They also buy locally grown produce, rather than fruits and vegetables that have been trucked several thousand miles, since conserving resources, including fuel, is an important goal of sustainable agriculture. For some parts of the country, this may mean forgoing certain crops during the winter.

Proponents of sustainable agriculture condemn herbicide-tolerant crops and are skeptical of genetic engineering in general. They fear that it will only strengthen current commercial farming practices. "We have two paths to the future," writes Nicanor Perlas, an international expert on sustainable agriculture. "We either pursue an ecological partnership with the living systems of our fragile planet or we assert our total rulership over the forces of nature and totally redesign our living environment through biotechnology."[13]

Future events will undoubtedly affect our social, philosophical, and environmental concerns regarding genetically engineered crops. If the new crops cause even one instance of serious environmental damage, resistance to genetic engineering could rise to new heights. On the other hand, as these crops become more familiar, public acceptance is likely to grow. A more knowledgeable public might also discriminate between the various new crops, accepting some while rejecting others. In the past, similar debate accompanied other developments in agriculture, including pasteurized milk, artificial insemination, and oleo margarine. Although once questioned, they are now accepted.

We can't say for certain how genetically engineered crops will affect the environment or change the life of farmers. If we could, it would be much, much easier for us to choose wisely and make up our own minds about whether to support the new technology. Lacking a crystal ball with which to read the future, we can only weigh the information available and draw conclusions as best we can.

-8-
FEEDING A HUNGRY WORLD

One of the most optimistic claims made for genetic engineering has been its potential to feed the world. Researchers have demonstrated that crops can be manipulated for increased yield and resistance to disease and insects. In theory, it would seem that such traits could be harnessed to serve the desperate need of hungry nations. Yet scientific advances alone cannot eliminate hunger in poor nations.

Eighteen million people, mostly children, die each year from starvation and malnutrition, according to a Johns Hopkins University study published in 1997. For many people, access to food is prevented by war or economic turmoil. The development of new crops will do little to solve their hunger crisis. If real progress is to be made, increased food production must be accompanied by political and economic change.[1]

Widespread hunger is expected to worsen as food production fails to keep pace with population growth. Experts estimate that the world's population will double by the year 2050, to 11 billion.[2]

Children clean up leftovers from a feeding pot in war-torn Rwanda. For many people, hunger is the result of war or economic turmoil.

Food production cannot keep up with this explosion. Although global population is expected to increase at a rate of 2 percent per year, food production is expected to increase at a rate of only 1 percent per year.

Experts agree that increasing the total number of acres devoted to farmland is not a realistic solution to this problem. Almost all land available for growing crops is already in use. Indeed, a key challenge is to stop modern development from encroaching upon farmland and taking fertile acres out of production.

For agricultural output to increase, the crops that are planted must yield more. Genetic engineering could play an important role in developing higher yielding varieties. Another way to increase yield is to decrease the amount of the harvest lost to insect pests or disease. Genetic modification has already shown its potential in this area. In theory, genetic engineering could also be used to develop new varieties of crops suited to less favorable soils and climates.

Have you ever seen the bumper sticker that says, EAT SIMPLY, THAT OTHERS MAY SIMPLY LIVE? Eating less meat and more vegetarian meals is one way to stretch scarce food resources. A large amount of grain is needed to fatten a steer. That same grain could be used to feed many people eating vegetarian meals. However, plant sources of protein are incomplete. They do not contain all the essential amino acids required by humans. To obtain complete proteins, people must combine different types of plants. (Eating peanut butter on a cracker, for instance, combines a legume with a cereal.) Unfortunately, a variety of plant crops is not available in all parts of the world. Genetically engineering crops for nutrition could help make a vegetarian diet more nutritionally complete.

Genetically engineered improvements like these could touch the lives of billions. Certainly science has staved off widespread starvation before. During the 1960s and 1970s, rice and wheat production in India, Pakistan, and the Philippines were greatly increased through the introduction of high-yielding hybrids and chemical fertilizers. This effort became known as the **Green Revolution.**

Genetic engineering, with its ability to transfer traits from one species to another, offers the promise of creating new plant varieties that cannot be developed through conventional means. Yet it's important to keep in mind that scientists from around the world, working together through an international network of research centers, were as important as the new hybrids to the success of the Green Revolution. A similar spirit of cooperation will be necessary to bring genetically engineered crops to poor nations.

Finally, it's also worth noting that not all advances in genetic engineering are necessarily good for impoverished nations. Indeed, some may actually worsen the plight of developing nations if they eliminate the need for important exports produced in those countries. The introduction of Calgene's genetically modified rapeseed is one example of this.

Calgene engineered rapeseed to produce laurate, an important ingredient in soap and food products, in its oil. Before this breakthrough, laurate was made from palm kernel and coconut oils. Such oils are only available from plants grown in the tropics. Their export was an important source of money to nations in Southeast Asia.[3] Calgene's new variety of rapeseed makes it much easier for industrialized nations to obtain laurate—and eliminates an important source of income for poor countries.

Feeding the world in 2050—or even 2005—is an immense undertaking. For developing countries to benefit from advances in genetic engineering, two major obstacles must be overcome. First, genetic scientists have paid scant attention to the food crops eaten by people in developing nations. Second, many important genetic engineering technologies were developed by companies that are unlikely to freely share their knowledge with poor countries.

Challenges to Solving
World Hunger with Genetics

Almost all of the anticipated world population growth—97 percent of it, in fact—will occur in the developing countries of Asia, Africa, and Latin America.[4] But the vast majority of genetic engineering research is being done in developed countries like the United States, France, Japan, and Australia. Crops that are important food sources in developing countries, such as **cassava**, sorghum, and millet, have received no attention from companies engaged in

Cassava is a tropical vegetable similar to a sweet potato. It is eaten by many people in Asia, Africa, and South America. Biotechnology companies are now working to develop improved varieties of this important food.

genetic engineering.[5] The reason is obvious: such crops are not big moneymakers in the United States and other industrialized countries. (Cassava is a tropical vegetable; sorghum is similar to corn; and millet describes several members of the grass family that are cultivated for cereal.)

Further research into crops important to the developing world is a first step toward meeting the needs of those countries. The next step is making those crops available. Unfortunately, poor nations lack the laboratories and trained scientists to conduct genetic engineering research. As a result, very little transgenics research is taking place in those nations. In the United States, 1,952 field trials of transgenic crops had been conducted by the end of 1995. By comparison, 78 had been conducted in Argentina; 60 in China; 38 in Mexico; and 1 in Zimbabwe.[6]

If research into transgenic crops for developing countries is going to take place, it will have to be the result of partnerships between the countries that have the technology and the countries that want it. This transfer of technology and information is much more likely for research conducted in government labs, universities, and other public institutions than for experiments performed by private companies. Only government and university scientists conduct research with the stated purpose of improving the public good. They expect to share their findings with other researchers. Making a profit is rarely part of their mission.

But many of the new varieties of genetically modified crops are owned by private companies like Monsanto and Novartis. The Biotechnology Industry Organization estimates that 80 percent of research into plant engineering is done by commercial companies.[7] To earn back the millions of dollars they have spent on research, such companies expect to sell their genetically engineered seeds for a profit. Other scientists who want to use their patented discoveries very often must pay a licensing fee. Understandably, for-profit companies are reluctant to share their seeds, even with agricultural centers in developing countries.

The solution to this problem is not just finding ways for poor countries to afford genetically engineered seeds. The long-term goal is to eliminate hunger and poverty through increased self-sufficiency. Simply shipping seeds to the developing world would make it even more dependent on industrialized nations. The answer, instead, is to create collaborations between nations. Ideally, such partnerships would offer equal benefits to each country.

Sharing Technology with Developing Nations

The International Laboratory for Tropical Agricultural Biotechnology, formed in 1991 as a partnership between the Scripps Research Institute (La Jolla, California) and ORSTOM, a French research institute, offers one model for the kind of collaboration needed to bring the promise of genetic engineering to developing countries. Scientists from India, China, Vietnam, and other countries visit the laboratory in La Jolla, California, to learn how to perform genetic engineering experiments. Funded by the Rockefeller Foundation, the laboratory is working to develop a virus-resistant cassava, among other research projects.

The International Service for the Acquisition of Agri-Biotech Applications (ISAAA), with offices in Kenya, England, Japan, and the United States, offers another model of cooperation between countries. ISAAA is trying to build links between company and university labs with transgenic technology and agricultural research centers in developing countries that can put the technology to use. ISAAA has targeted national agricultural programs in 12 countries in Asia, Africa, and Latin America for participation. Its sponsors include companies like Monsanto, Pioneer Hi-Bred, Novartis, and philanthropies like the McKnight Foundation and the Rockefeller Foundation.

In ISAAA's first project, in 1992, Monsanto gave Mexican scientists virus-resistant genes for potatoes. With these genes, the Mexican scientists could develop transgenic potato varieties that would be grown by poor farmers. In exchange, the Mexican scientists introduced Monsanto to a number of unfamiliar potato varieties grown locally in Mexico.[8] This introduction was potentially useful to Monsanto because the company could investigate the new varieties for useful genes. Several other ISAAA projects have included a partnership among Cornell University, Brazil, and Thailand that will develop virus-resistant papaya; a collaboration between Sandoz (now Novartis) and several Latin American countries to study cassava; and an agreement between Asgrow and the University of Costa Rica to develop virus-resistant melons.

In Zurich, Switzerland, scientists at the Swiss Federal Institute of Technology and the University of Freiburg in Germany are working together to create a variety of transgenic rice that is a good source of vitamin A. If rice, which is a staple throughout most of Asia, had the enzymes needed to produce vitamin A, the rate of the disease xerophthalmia, which can cause blindness, could be greatly reduced. This European team used a gene gun to add genes from bacteria and a variety of daffodil to create their new rice. When the rice is ready for planting, it will be distributed through the International Rice Research Institute in Manila, the Philippines.[9]

Projects like these are still in the early stages. Hopefully, such efforts will turn the promise of genetic engineering into a reality. Without combining good science with good intentions and honest collaboration, it will be impossible to meet the nutritional needs of the next century.

-9-
THE FUTURE
OF GENETICALLY
ENGINEERED FOODS

What would be your reaction if you were sitting at a restaurant and your waiter handed you this menu?

A Dinner of Transgenic Foods[1]

Appetizers

Spiced Potatoes with Waxmoth gene
Juice of Tomatoes with Flounder gene

Entree

Blackened Catfish with Trout gene
Scalloped Potatoes with Chicken gene
Cornbread with Firefly gene

Dessert

Rice Pudding with Pea gene

Beverage

Milk from Bovine Growth Hormone (BGH)-
Supplemented Cows

You'd be rather surprised, no doubt! This unusual menu was published by the National Wildlife Federation in 1991 to draw attention to genetically engineered foods. At that time, BGH had not yet received approval for commercial use. Scientists were conducting experiments with the other transgenic foods mentioned, but only the catfish with a trout gene ever approached commercial sale. Still, the menu effectively illustrated the scope of research in transgenic foods. Since the National Wildlife Federation was opposed to genetically engineered food, it was no accident that the menu selections were designed to sound as unappealing and unnatural as possible.

Now take a look at this list of foods:

- Milk with the flavor and thickness of whole milk, but only a fraction of the cholesterol

- High-quality, aged cheese made with enzymes developed through biotechnology

- Sweeter carrots

- Crisper celery

- Low-cholesterol beef

These fanciful foods appear in a handout written and distributed by the Biotechnology Industry Organization. According to the brochure, foods like these are what you might see during a trip to the supermarket in the twenty-first century. The Biotechnology Industry Organization represents more than 600 biotechnology companies, academic institutions, and state biotechnology centers. Obviously, the Biotechnology Industry Organization wants the public to have a positive attitude toward genetically engineered foods. For this reason, its shopping list emphasizes the potential improvements genetic modification could bring to food in terms of taste and nutrition.

The use of fictional menus and shopping lists like these is one way that a group can attempt to sway public sentiment. By creating a fictional supermarket or restaurant of the future, an organization can easily make genetically engineered foods sound either appealing or frightening.

Since the future offers an unlimited smorgasbord of possibilities, the organization can be quite selective about the foods it wishes to emphasize. Want to make genetically engineered food sound like a great idea? Talk about sweeter carrots or low-cholesterol pork. Want to make it sound scary and weird? Mention corn with a chicken gene.

Of course, such scenes of the future are rooted in today's laboratory experiments. Still, the path from research lab to supermarket shelf is strewn with obstacles. There is no guarantee that one specific product will ever make it to market. For this reason, it's very difficult to predict what particular items a "Feast of the Future" might actually include.

Nevertheless, taking the long view of such experiments can offer a glimpse at what the next decades might bring. Trends that are firmly rooted in the present are likely to extend into the future. Obviously, genetically engineered crops that are popular and profitable today are quite likely to be successful in the future.

Future Trends

The first 2 years that genetically manipulated crops were commercially grown crops—1996 and 1997—clearly demonstrated that they were here to stay. More and more acreage is expected to be planted with crops engineered for insect and herbicide resistance. In fact, company officials at Pioneer Hi-Bred expect transgenic crops to account for one-third to one-half of their seedlings by the year 2000.[2] Crops engineered for resistance to other types of herbicides, especially glufosinate, are right around the corner. So are more types of crops engineered with Bt genes for resistance to insect pests.

Although the first crop engineered for disease-resistance, the Freedom II squash, was approved in 1995, no crop has followed it to commercialization. Still, though this research area is growing rather slowly, several disease-resistant crops were in the pipeline toward government approval in late 1997. They included a new version of the Freedom II squash, one engineered for resistance against three viruses instead of two, a virus-resistant grape from DNA Plant Technology, and a virus-resistant potato from Cornell University.[3] Disease-resistant crops are potentially lucrative and should attract more attention in future years.

Research into other types of genetically altered crops that offer increased profitability to the farmer is expected to continue. This includes developing crops that can grow in poor soils and harsh climates. It also includes designing cereal crops that can draw nitrogen from the soil and the air. (This is called "fixing" nitrogen.) Nitrogen, an element plants need to grow, is an important component of plant fertilizer.

Plants with a gene for **nitrogen fixation** would reduce the farmer's need for fertilizer.

Livestock animals engineered to produce pharmaceutical proteins in their milk or blood will probably remain a very active area of investigation, and research into livestock modified for growth qualities is likely to become more intensive. Modified milk, for example, promises to be an especially fruitful area of research. By engineering cow milk to be more like human milk, it will become possible to develop new products for babies, the elderly, and immune-compromised people.

Other possibilities for the future include engineering microorganisms for use in food processing and manufacturing. Microorganisms—bacteria, yeasts, and molds—play an essential role in aging cheese, fermenting wine and beer, and baking bread. Engineered microorganisms could be designed to improve the production and quality of these products.

Food spoilage and contamination is currently an enormous problem. Recombinant DNA technology could be used to develop faster and more sensitive methods for identifying and locating toxins, pathogens, and other food contaminants.

New types of vegetable oils used for cooking and food manufacturing are also being investigated. Genetic engineering could change the composition of these oils for a variety of purposes. Shoppers would appreciate oils with lower cholesterol, while food manufacturers could use the new oils in various processed products.

The first wave of genetically engineered crops had traits that appealed to the farmer. The next wave of crops, experts predict, will have characteristics designed to appeal to shoppers.[4] Genetically engineered crops of the future will affect taste, appearance, texture, and aroma, they say. The technology could also be used to develop naturally sweet or salty varieties of plants. But this research isn't just about developing better-tasting spinach. Imagine yogurt that doesn't get watery or potato chips without dark streaks! These are just two possible improvements through genetic modification.[5]

Functional Foods

One of the most interesting predictions for the future involves the application of genetically engineered food to the health field. In a few laboratories, scientists are working to develop vegetables and fruits that could be used as vehicles for delivering vaccines against disease.[6]

Foods are also being examined for their nutritional components. Foods that provide a health benefit beyond meeting ordinary nutritional needs are often called **functional foods**. They have also been called designer foods, nutraceuticals, and pharmafoods. Although the field is in its infancy, the potential of using recombinant DNA technology to boost the health benefits of food is irresistible to many. This is where the average person is most likely to benefit from genetically modified foods. The first such food, a carrot engineered for extra beta-carotene, became commercially available in Texas in early 1998.

The Betasweet carrot, developed by scientists at Texas A& M University's Vegetable Improvement Center, debuted in January 1998 in Houston supermarkets. The novel maroon carrot contained no foreign genes. Instead, one of its own genes was engineered to produce high levels of beta-carotene, a nutrient thought to prevent several types of cancer. *The Houston Chronicle* called it the "first of what promises to be a number of super vegetables."[7]

Foods that contain substances thought to prevent disease have attracted enormous attention in recent years from both the public and the scientific community. These fruits and vegetables have always been a part of the human diet and some of them, like garlic, have a long association with disease prevention. What's new is that scientists have begun investigating the disease-preventing components of such foods. These components are known as **phytochemicals.** (Phytochemical means "plant chemical.") Beta-carotene is one phytochemical. As scientists have identified more phytochemicals, consumer demand for foods high in these substances has grown. Food industry experts predict that new fruit and vegetable varieties will be developed that contain high levels of phytochemicals.

Interest in foods that prevent disease began when scientists noticed that countries where people eat a diet rich in vegetables and fruit have substantially lower rates of many kinds of cancer. Studies done since then have confirmed the link between diet and cancer. Indeed, the National Cancer Institute estimates that 1 in 3 cancer deaths are diet related, and that 8 of 10 cancers have a diet component.[8] Apparently the old saying is true: "You are what you eat!" To reduce our risk of cancer, we're told to cut down on fat and boost our fiber by eating at least five helpings of fruits and vegetables each day.

So what substances should get the credit for fighting cancer? In 1989, the National Cancer Institute set out to answer just that question by funding a new program within its Division of Cancer Prevention and Control. Thousands of food components were identified as possible phytochemicals with cancer preventing qualities. Although the investigation is far from over, here are some early standouts:

- Broccoli, cauliflower, brussels sprouts, kale, and other vegetables in the cabbage family. These vegetables are rich in a sulforaphane, a compound that stimulates the body to produce enzymes that prevent tumor growth. They're also a good source of fiber.[9]

- Tomatoes, red peppers, and red grapefruit contain lycopene, a substance associated with the prevention of several types of cancer.[10]

- Garlic contains allylic sulfides, which enhance immune function.

- Carrots and other yellow and dark green vegetables contain high amounts of beta-carotene. Beta-carotene was long believed to help prevent cancer, although recent studies indicate it might be less potent than once thought.

It might seem that if we could identify a food's key nutrient or nutrients, we could bottle it as a kind of supervitamin. But what scientists suspect is that phytochemicals work most effectively when they are eaten in their natural form—as part of carrot or kale. Whether that's due to some complex interaction of compounds or some as yet unidentified key components remains to be seen. The result, however, has been a tremendous interest in building better vegetables.

No single food has been found to prevent cancer—and it's unlikely that one will be. It seems that eating a variety of whole foods is the best way to obtain all the substances necessary for good health. Scientists still have a long way to go toward understanding how phytochemicals work—and work together—in the human body. This is why the modification of whole foods has attracted attention. A person eating a fruit or vegetable modified to contain a larger amount of a particular phytochemical would gain the benefits not only of that substance but also of all the other beneficial components and fiber in the food as well.

Genetic engineering may one day be used to boost the beneficial properties of food. It could do this in two ways. It might be used to make the fruit or vegetable more nutritious, like the Betasweet carrot. Or it might simply make the food tastier or otherwise more appealing to eat. People would then eat more of it and thus get more of its nutrients, or so the thinking goes.

Genetically modified crops have taken enormous strides in the past decade, and many technical difficulties in their development have been overcome. Yet making a new food means more than simply designing new seeds. It involves selling those seeds to farmers. It means harvesting the produce and shipping it to market successfully. And it means finding shoppers who are willing to buy the new food. Members of the public—like you—will continue to play an important role in the development of new genetically engineered foods.

GLOSSARY

Agrobacterium tumefaciens—a soil bacterium that produces crown gall disease in some plants. Scientists use a mutant form of the bacterium to transfer genes into plants.

amino acid—a building block of protein.

antibiotic—a substance derived from a microorganism that can inhibit or kill a foreign bacterium.

artificial insemination—the placement of sperm directly into a female's vagina, cervix, or uterus using a plastic tube or syringe.

***Bacillus thuringiensis* (Bt)**—a soil bacterium that produces a protein toxic to leaf-eating insects. The Bt protein is harmless to people, birds, animals, and some beneficial insects.

bioreactor—in genetic engineering, a transgenic animal that produces pharmaceutical products.

biotechnology—the development of products by any biological process, including recombinant DNA technology, fermentation, and embryo rescue. Frequently used as if it were a synonym for recombinant DNA technology.

bovine somatotropin (BST)—a growth hormone naturally produced in the pituitary gland of cattle. Injections of the hormone improve milk production in cows. Also called bovine growth hormone (BGH).

cassava—a tropical vegetable like a large yam.

chromosome—a rod-shaped structure, consisting of

123

DNA and proteins, that is present in every cell nucleus. Each chromosome contains thousands of genes.

chymosin—an enzyme used in cheese-making. Bacteria, yeasts, and fungi have been genetically engineered to produce chymosin.

clone—an identical copy.

DNA (deoxyribonucleic acid)—the molecule that carries genetic heritage. DNA is a two-stranded molecule twisted into a double helix. DNA is sometimes referred to as genetic material.

differentiate—in science, to becomes a particular kind of cell. Traditionally, scientists have believed that once a cell differentiates, its destiny is set and it cannot become any other kind of cell.

electroporation—using small surges of electricity to create small holes in cell membranes so that foreign DNA can pass through.

embryo rescue—the process of crossing two plant varieties that ordinarily will not breed.

enzyme—a type of protein that controls chemical reactions.

Escherichia coli (E. coli)—a bacterium that inhabits the intestinal tract of vertebrates.

ethylene gas—a chemical sprayed on tomatoes and other fruits and vegetables that are picked while they are still green. The gas make the foods look ripe.

functional food—a food that provides a health benefit beyond meeting ordinary nutritional needs.

gene—a segment of DNA that contains the blueprint for a protein. Through the action of their proteins, genes govern inherited traits like physical appearance.

gene gun—device used to shoot microscopic pellets coated with DNA into cells.

genetic engineer—a scientist who conducts research using the methods of recombinant DNA technology.

genetic engineering—see **recombinant DNA technology**.

genetic material—see **DNA**.

genome—a complete set of all the genes of an organism.

genomic mapping—creating a visual representation that explains the relationship between DNA segments on an organism's chromosomes.

Green Revolution—a successful effort in the 1960s and 1970s to increase wheat and rice production in India, Pakistan, and the Philippines through new high-yielding hybrids and chemical fertilizers.

herbicide—a weed-killing chemical. Examples include glufosinate or glyphosate.

host organism—in genetic engineering, the creature that receives the altered gene.

hybrid—the offspring of parents that are genetically different.

hybridization—the process of joining two complimentary strands of DNA.

inbreeding—to allow plants to self-pollinate or animals to mate with close relatives for several generations.

kanamycin—an antibiotic that has been used in gene transfer as a marker gene.

laurate—a key raw material used in the manufacture of processed foods.

ligase—an enzyme used to join DNA segments together.

microinjection—a technique used to introduce DNA into an egg cell using a very small needle.

microorganism—an organism so small that it can be seen only with a microscope.

nitrogen fixation—the process of taking nitrogen from the air and converting it into a nutrient necessary for plant growth.

nucleotide—a single unit of DNA, consisting of a sugar, a phosphate, and one of four bases.

pesticide—a chemical used to kill insects or other pests.

pharming—raising transgenic livestock that produce pharmaceutical products.

phytochemicals—naturally occurring chemicals found in vegetables and fruit that help prevent disease.

rapeseed—a plant in the mustard family. The oil of the rapeseed is canola oil.

recombinant DNA technology (rDNA)—techniques used to manipulate DNA segments in the laboratory to form novel organisms. Popularly called genetic engineering or genetic modification. See also **transgenic**.

restriction enzyme—an enzyme that cuts DNA at specific locations.

selective breeding—actively choosing which animals or plants will be allowed to breed.

somaclonal variation—the process of looking for natural mutations in single plant cells and then growing those cells into new plants.

splice—to insert a foreign gene into an organism's DNA.

sustainable agriculture—agricultural practices, such as avoiding chemical pesticides and herbicides, that are intended to keep the land productive for future generations.

totipotent—an undifferentiated cell that is capable of developing into a new organism.

transgenic—an organism that contains DNA from another species. Recombinant DNA technology is used to create transgenic organisms.

END NOTES

Introduction

1. Seabrook, John. "Tremors in the Hothouse." *New Yorker.* July 19, 1993, p. 33.

2. Pollack, Andrew. "Test Is Due Today on Gene Altering." *New York Times.* May 30, 1986, p. A15.

Chapter 1

1. Maryanski, J. H. "U.S. Food and Drug Administration Policy for Foods Developed by Biotechnology," in *Genetically Modified Foods: Safety Issues,* edited by Karl-Heinz Engel, Gary R. Takeoka, and Roy Teranishi. (Washington, DC: American Chemical Society, 1995).

Chymosin made by Pfizer Central Research (New York, NY) with genetically engineered *E. coli* bacteria (Chy-Max) was approved in March 1990. Chymosin made by Genencor International (South San Francisco, CA) with genetically engineered fungi (Chymogen) was approved in May 1993 and is the source of the chymosin derived from genetic engineering in use today, according to the Biotechnology Industry Organization (Washington, DC).

2. Biotechnology Industry Organization. *BIO Editors' and Reporters' Guide to Biotechnology.* 1996–1997.

3. Baumgardt, Bill R. and Marshall A. Martin, coeditors. *Agricultural Biotechnology Issues and Choices.* West Lafayette, IN: Purdue University Agricultural Experiment Station, 1991, p.139.

4. Interview on March 11, 1997 with associate professor Gary D. Schnitkey, Department of Agricultural Economics and Rural Sociology, in his office at Ohio State University.

5. Traynor, Pat. "Whither the Flavr Savr?" *ISB News Report.* March 1996; King, R. T. "Low-Tech Woe Slows Calgene's Super Tomato." *Wall Street Journal.* April 11, 1996, p. B1.

6. Denny, Sharon. "What Will You Be Eating in the 21st Century?" *Current Health.* September 1995, p. 25.

Chapter 2

1. Lyon, Jeff and Peter Gorner. *Altered Fates: The Genetic Reengineering of Human Life.* New York: W. W. Norton & Company, 1994, p. 57; Micklos, David A. and Greg A. Freyer. *DNA Science: A First Course in Recombinant DNA Technology.* Burlington, North Carolina: Cold Spring Harbor Laboratory Press and Carolina Biological Supply Company, 1990, p. 42.

2. Palmiter, R. D. et al. "Dramatic growth of mice that develop from eggs microinjected with metallothionein-growth hormone fusion genes." *Nature.* v. 300, 1982, p. 611—615.

Chapter 3

My interview with associate professor L. Mark Lagrimini, Department of Horticulture, Ohio State University, in his office on March 13, 1997 contributed to my understanding of gene transfer in plants.

1. Cohen, Jon. "Corn Genome Pops Out of the Pack." *Science.* June 27, 1997, p. 1962.

2. Cohen, ibid.

3. Phillips, Susan C. "Genetically engineered foods: Do they pose health and environmental hazards?" *CQ Researcher.* v. 4, n. 29, August 5, 1994, p. 683.

4. Baumgardt, Bill R. and Marshall A. Martin. *Agricultural Biotechnology: Issues and Choices.* West Lafayette, IN: Purdue University Agricultural Experiment Station, 1991, p. 12.

5. Interview with professor James D. Murray, Department of Animal Science, University of California, Davis, on February 3, 1997.

Chapter 4

1. Pollack, Andrew. "Test Is Due Today on Gene Altering." *New York Times.* May 30, 1986, p. A15.

2. James, Clive and Anatole F. Krattiger. *Global Review of the Field Testing and Commercialization of Transgenic Plants: 1986–1995.* International Service for the Acquisition of Agri-biotech Applications. Ithaca, New York: 1996, p. 5.

3. Myerson, Allen R. "Field of Genes." *New York Times,* November 19, 1997.

4. Weiss, Rick. "New Variety of Corn Reaps Controversy." *Washington Post.* October 8, 1996.

5. Madden, Dean. *Food Biotechnology: An Introduction.* Brussels, Belgium: ILSI Europe Concise Monograph Series, 1995, p. 18.

6. Phillips, Susan C. "Genetically engineered foods: Do they pose health and environmental hazards?" *CQ Researcher.* v. 4, n. 29, August 5, 1994. See also quotes from Margaret Mellon, director of the National Biotechnology Policy Center of the National Wildlife Federation, in John Seabrook's article "Tremors in the Hothouse." *New Yorker.* July 19, 1993, p. 36.

7. Benson, Susan, Mark Arax, and Rachel Burstein. "A Growing Concern." *Mother Jones.* January/February 1997, p. 40.

8. Charry, Tamar. "Monsanto Recruits the Horticulturist of the San Diego Zoo to Pitch its Popular Herbicide." *New York Times.* May 29, 1997.

9. "What's Coming to Market." *Gene Exchange.* Fall 1997.

10. Westwood, Jim. "Growers Endorse Herbicide Resistance, Recognize Need for Responsible Use," *ISB News Report.* March 1997.

11. Pszczola, Donald E. "Activists Target Transgenic Soybeans." *Food Technology.* November 1996, p. 29.

12. "1997 Global Acreage of Monsanto's Transgenic Crops." *Gene Exchange.* Fall 1997.

13. "Genetically Engineered Virus Resistant Squash Approved for Sale." *TSTR News Report.* January 1995.

14. "Post-Approval Blues." *Gene Exchange.* Fall 1997.

15. Blowers, Jay S. "High Starch Crops on the Horizon." *ISB News Report.* November 1992.

16. "What's Coming to Market?" *Gene Exchange.* Fall 1997; Also information from Calgene's World Wide Web page. The address for the web page is **www.calgene.com/corporate**.

17. Myerson, Allen R. "Monsanto Settling Genetic Seed Complaints." *New York Times.* February 24, 1998, p. C2.

Chapter 5

My interview with professor James Murray, Department of Animal Science and Department of Population Health and Reproduction, University of California, Davis, on February 3, 1997 contributed to my understanding of gene transfer in animals.

1. "Mighty Mice; Gene Transfers Create Giants." *Time.* December 27, 1982, p. 79.

2. The conference "Transgenic Animals in Agriculture," was sponsored by the University of California, Davis, and held in Tahoe City, California, August 24–27, 1997.

3. Wall, R. J. et al. "Transgenic Dairy Cattle: Genetic Engineering on a Large Scale." *Journal of Dairy Science,* v. 80, n. 9, September 1997, 2213–2224.

4. Gibbons, Anne M. Summary of her talk "Blastodermal Chimeras as a Route to Transgenic Chickens," in Transgenic Animals in Agriculture conference program, p. 19.

5. Madden, Dean. *Food Biotechnology: An Introduction.* Brussels, Belgium: ILSI Europe Concise Monograph Series, 1995, p. 24.

6. Phillips, Susan C. "Genetically engineered foods: Do they pose health and environmental hazards?" *CQ Researcher.* v. 4, n. 29, August 5, 1994.

7. Madden, ibid.

8. Lau, Edie. "Cloned Sheep Dolly Only the Start, Researchers Say." *Sacramento Bee.* August 26, 1997, p. A1.

9. Mench, Joy A. Summary of her talk "Animal Welfare Concerns and Transgenic Farm Animals," in Transgenic Animals in Agriculture conference program, p. 30.

10. Specter, Michael and Gina Kolata. "After Decades and Many Missteps, Cloning Success." *New York Times.* March 3, 1997, p. A8.

11. Cooper, Julian. "Protein Production in Transgenic Animals," *Agricultural Biotechnology: Novel Products and New Partnerships,* NABC Report 8, Ithaca, NY, 1996.

12. Wilmut, I. et al. "Viable offspring derived from fetal and adult mammalian cells." *Nature.* February 27, 1997, pp. 810–813.

13. Goldberg, Carey and Gina Kolata. "Scientists Announce Births of Cows Cloned in New Way." *New York Times.* January 21, 1998, p. A14.

14. Specter, ibid.

15. Specter, ibid.

Chapter 6
1. Henkel, John. "Genetic Engineering: Fast Forwarding to Future Foods." *FDA Consumer.* April 1995, p. 6.

2. Hopkins, D. Douglas, Rebecca J. Goldburg, and Steven A. Hirsch. *A Mutable Feast: Assuring Food Safety in the Era of Genetic Engineering.* New York: Environmental Defense Fund, 1991.

3. International Food Information Council World Wide Web site at **http://ificinfo.health.org.**

4. U.S. Food and Drug Administration. "Statement of policy: foods derived from new plant varieties." *Federal Register.* May 29, 1992, pp. 22984–23005.

5. Nordlee, J. A. et al. "Identification of a Brazil-nut allergen in transgenic soybeans," *New England Journal of Medicine.* v. 334 n. 11, March 14, 1996, pp. 668–92.

6. Phillips, Susan C. "Genetically Engineered Foods: Do They Pose Health and Environmental Hazards?" *CQ Researcher.* August 5, 1994, v. 4 n. 29 p. 675; also Baumgardt, Bill R. and Marshall A. Martin. *Agricultural Biotechnology.* West Lafayette, IN: Purdue University Agricultural Experiment Station, 1991, p. 62.

7. Phillips, ibid.

8. Baumgardt, ibid. p. 61.

9. International Food Information Council press release "New Survey Reveals U.S. Consumer Confidence in Food Biotechnology . . ." It can be read on IFIC's World Wide Web site. **http://ificinfo.health.org/press/**.

10. Feder, Barnaby J. "Biotechnology Company to Join Those Urging Labels on Genetically Altered Products." *New York Times.* February 24, 1997.

11. From Ben & Jerry's World Wide Web site: **http://www.benjerry.com**.

12. Phillips, ibid. p. 687.

13. Berselli, Beth. "Settlement Reached in Hormone Labeling Case." *Washington Post.* August 15, 1997, p. A22.

Chapter 7

1. Burros, Marian. "Eating Well: Trying to Get Labels on Genetically Engineered Food." *New York Times.* May 21, 1997.

2. Hoban, Thomas J. "Consumer Acceptance of Biotechnology: An International Perspective." *Nature Biotechnology.* March 15, 1997, pp. 232–234.

3. The presentation, given in California and Indiana, was described to me by Christine M. Bruhn, director of the Center for Consumer Research, at the University of California, Davis, during an interview in her office on February 3, 1997. The title of the video is *Biotechnology, A Better Understanding.*

4. Chargoff, Erwin. "On the Dangers of Genetic Meddling." *Science.* v. 192, 1976, pp. 938–940.

5. Rifkin's press release appears in an article by Susan C. Phillips titled "Genetically Engineered Foods: Do They Pose Health and Envirnomental Hazards?" *CQ Researcher.* August 5, 1994, p. 687.

6. Interview with Bruhn, ibid.

7. Bruhn, Christine M. et al. Information booklet titled "Most Commonly Asked Questions about Food Biotechnology," printed by the University of California, p. 6.

8. Sudduth, Mary Alice. "Genetically Engineered Foods: Fears & Facts." *FDA Consumer.* Jan/Feb 1993.

9. For example, Environmental Defense Fund scientist Rebecca Goldburg is quoted as saying, "I think a lot of people just don't feel right in their gut about recombinant DNA in agriculture—they feel on some level it's not right to mix plant and animal genes. But, unfortunately, health concerns are the only mechanism available to them to express their doubts. We have to talk about whether these products are safe, not whether they are necessary or desirable." Seabrook, John. "Tremors in the Hothouse." *New Yorker.* July 19, 1993, p. 37.

10. Baumgardt, Bill R. and Marshall A. Martin. *Agricultural Biotechnology: Issues and Choices.* West Lafayette, IN: Purdue University Agricultural Experiment Station, 1991, p. 131.

11. Sorensen, A. Ann. "Farmer Concerns: Food Safety, Biotechnology, and the Consumer," p. 115. Chapter in *National Agricultural Biotechnology Council-2.* June

Fessenden MacDonald, editor. Ithaca, NY: National Agricultural Biotechnology Council, 1990.

12. Union of Concerned Scientists briefing paper on "Sustainable Agriculture." Written by Margaret Mellon, Jane Rissler, and Freya McCamant of UCS's Agriculture and Biotechnology Program. The paper can be read on the World Wide Web at http://www.ucsusa.org.

13. Perlas, Nicanor. *Overcoming Illusions About Biotechnology.* London and New Jersey: Zed Books, 1994, p. 107.

Chapter 8
1. Groves, Martha. "Plant Researchers Offer Bumper Crop of Humanity." *Los Angeles Times.* Fifth article in a five-part series on world hunger. December 26, 1997, p. A1.

2. James, C. and A. F. Krattiger. *Global Review of the Field Testing and Commercialization of Transgenic Plants. 1986 to 1995: The First Decade of Crop Biotechnology.* ISAAA (International Service for the Acquisition of Agri-Biotech Applications) Briefs, No. 1. Ithaca, NY: ISAAA, 1996, p. 1

3. Schmidt, Karen. "Whatever Happened to the Gene Revolution?" *New Scientist.* January 7, 1995, p. 24.

4. James, ibid.

5. Baumgardt, Bill R. and Marshall A. Martin. *Agricultural Biotechnology: Issues and Choices.* Purdue University Agricultural Experiment Station. West Lafayette, IN: 1991, p. 116.

6. James, ibid. p. 5

7. Biotechnology Industry Organization. *The Transfer of Agricultural Biotechnology to Developing Countries.* Washington, DC, 1996, p. 1.

8. Schmidt, ibid.

9. Prakash, C. S. "Towards High Provitamin-A Rice." *ISB News Report.* August 1997.

Chapter 9

1. This menu appeared in the newsletter *The Gene Exchange: A Public Voice on Genetic Engineering.* v. 2, n. 4. December 1991, p. 1. At that time, the newsletter was published by the National Biotechnology Center of the National Wildlife Federation. Since 1994, it has been published by the Union of Concerned Scientists.

2. Feder, Barnaby J. "Out of the Lab, A Revolution on the Farm." *New York Times.* March 3, 1996.

3. "What's in the Commercial Pipeline?" *ISB News Report.* March 1998.

4. The predictions described in this paragraph and those that follow are drawn from three sources:

- Katz, Fran. "Biotechnology—New Tools in Food Technology's Toolbox." *Food Technology.* November 1996, pp. 63–66.

- Lacy, Bill, et al. Food Industry workshop report appearing in *National Agricultural Biotechnology Council Report-8.* Hardy, Ralph W. F. and Jane Baker Segelken, editors. Ithaca, NY: National Agricultural Biotechnology Council, 1996, p. 33.

- Thomas, Paul R. and Robert Earl, editors. Committee on Opportunities in the Nutrition and Food Sciences. Institute Medicine. *Opportunities in the Nutrition and Food Sciences.* Washington, DC: National Academy Press, 1994, pp. 128–140.

5. Phillips, Susan C. "Genetically Engineered Foods: Do They Pose Health and Environmental Hazards?" *CQ Researcher.* August 5, 1994, p. 675.

6. Arntzen, Charles J. "Crop Biotechnology in the Service of Medical and Veterinary Science," pp. 107–114. Article in *National Agricultural Biotechnology Council Report-8.* Hardy, Ralph W. F. and Jane Baker Segelken, editors. Ithaca, NY:

National Agricultural Biotechnology Council, 1996; Uhlman, Marian. "Creating a New Reason to Eat Vegetables." *Philadelphia Inquirer.* October 6, 1997, p. D1.

7. Antosh, Nelson. "Aggie-colored Carrot Debuting Here." *Houston Chronicle.* January 27, 1998, Business section, p. 7.

8. The American Dietetic Association. "Phytochemicals and Functional Foods." *Journal of the American Dietetic Association.* v. 95, 1995, p. 493.

9. Jaret, Peter. "Foods in a Pill." *Health.* March 1998, p. 89.

10. International Food Information Council World Wide Web page **http://ificinfo.health.org** "Backgrounder: Functional Foods."

FOR FURTHER INFORMATION

Magazine Articles

Berselli, Beth. "Settlement Reached in Hormone Labeling Case." *Washington Post*, August 15, 1997, p. A22

Burros, Marian. "Eating Well: Trying to Get Labels on Genetically Altered Food." *New York Times*. May 21, 1997, p. B8

Denny, Sharon. "What Will You Be Eating in the 21st Century?" *Current Health*. September 1995, p. 25.

Feder, Barnaby J. "Biotechnology Company to Join Those Urging Labels on Genetically Altered Products." *New York Times*. February 24, 1997.

Goldberg, Carey and Gina Kolata. "Scientists Announce Births of Cows Cloned in New Way." *New York Times*. January 21, 1998, p. A14.

Graves, Jacqueline M. "Designer Genes for Your Plate." *Fortune*. July 10, 1995, p. 22.

Groves, Martha. "Plant Researchers Offer Bumper Crop of Humanity." *Los Angeles Times*. Fifth article in a five-part series on world hunger. December 26, 1997, p. A1.

Ibrahim, Youssef M. "Genetic Soybeans Alarm Europeans." *New York Times*. November 7, 1996.

Jaret, Peter. "Foods in a Pill." *Health*. March 1998, p. 89.

Katz, Fran. "Biotechnology—New Tools in Food Technology's Toolbox." *Food Technology*. November 1996, pp. 63–66.

Kummer, Corby. "Building Better Veggies." *Self*. February 1996, pp. 145–151.

"Mighty Mice; Gene Transfers Create Giants." *Time*. December 27, 1982, p. 79.

Myerson, Allen R. "Field of Genes." *New York Times*. November 19, 1997.

————. "Monsanto Settling Genetic Seed Complaints." *New York Times.* February 24, 1998, p. C2.

Pollack, Andrew. "Test is Due Today on Gene Altering." *New York Times.* May 30, 1986, p. A15.

Schmidt, Karen. "Whatever Happened to the Gene Revolution?" *New Scientist.* January 7, 1995, p. 21.

Seabrook, John. "Tremors in the Hothouse." *New Yorker.* July 19, 1993, p. 32.

Specter, Michael and Gina Kolata. "After Decades and Many Missteps, Cloning Success." *New York Times.* March 3, 1997, p. A8.

Weiss, Rick. "New Variety of Corn Reaps Controversy." *Washington Post.* October 8, 1996.

Books

Agricultural Research Service Information Staff. *Science in Your Shopping Cart.* Greenbelt, Maryland: U.S. Department of Agriculture, March 1996.

Baumgardt, Bill R. and Marshall A. Martin. *Agricultural Biotechnology: Issues and Choices.* West Lafayette, IN: Purdue University Agricultural Experiment Station, 1991.

Doyle, Jack. *Altered Harvest.* New York: Viking, 1985.

Engel, Karl-Heinz, Gary R. Takeoka and Roy Teranishi, editors. *Genetically Modified Foods: Safety Issues.* Washington, D.C.: American Chemical Society, 1995. See especially Chapter 2, "U.S. Food and Drug Administration Policy for Foods Developed by Biotechnology," by J. H. Maryanski, p. 12.

Hopkins, D. Douglas, Rebecca J. Goldburg, and Steven A. Hirsch. *A Mutable Feast: Assuring Food Safety in the Era of Genetic Engineering.* New York: Environmental Defense Fund, 1991.

Mather, Robin. *Garden of Unearthly Delights.* New York: Dutton, 1995.

Perlas, Nicanor. *Overcoming Illusions about Biotechnology.* London: Zed Books, 1994.

Reiss, Michael J. and Roger Straughan. *Improving Nature? The Science and Ethics of Genetic Engineering,* Cambridge: Cambridge University Press. 1996.

Internet Resources

The address for Ben & Jerry's is **www.benjerry.com**. Click on the Ben & Jerry's rBGH policy statement.

The address for Calgene is **www.calgene.com.** Click on "Oils Division," "Cotton Division," and "Fresh Produce" for information on Calgene's genetically engineered products.

The address for the Centers for Consumer Research is **drinc.ucdavis.edu/CCR/**. Click on "Biotechnology."

The address for the Food and Drug Administration's Center for Food Safety and Applied Nutrition is **vm.cfsan.fda.gov**. Click on "Biotechnology."

The address for the International Food Information Council is **www.ificinfo.health.org**.

For general information about Monsanto Company, try **www.monsanto.com**. For more specific information, try **www.RoundupReady.com/soybeans/**. Click on "Technology Overview" for information on genetically engineered products. You can learn more about Posilac at **www.monsanto.com/dairy/**. Click on "Technical Information."

The address for the Pure Food Campaign is **www.geocities.com/athens/1527**.

To reach the U.S. Department of Agriculture's Biotechnology Information Center, type **www.nal.usda.gov/bic/**. To reach the Animal and Plant Health Inspection Service, go to **www.aphis.usda.gov**. Click on "Ag Biotechnology" to reach APHIS biotechnology newsletter and fact sheet.

INDEX

143

ABOUT THE AUTHOR

Elizabeth L. Marshall was born in Minneapolis, Minnesota, but grew up in southern California and New York City suburbs. She graduated from the University of Virginia with a B.A. in English and from the University of Pittsburgh with an M.F.A. in fiction writing. Ms. Marshall has been on the staff of *McCall's* magazine, the *Amherst Bulletin*, and *The Scientist.* She is a member of the National Association of Science Writers. Her first book, *The Human Genome Project: Cracking the Code within Us*, was published by Franklin Watts in 1996, and her second book, *Conquering Infertility: Medical Challenges and Moral Dilemmas*, was published by Franklin Watts in 1997. Ms. Marshall and her husband, Jeff Seiken, live in Columbus, Ohio, with their two young daughters.